The art of
SCREEN PRINTING

The art of
SCREEN PRINTING

ANTHONY KINSEY

B T BATSFORD LIMITED   LONDON

First published 1979
ISBN 0 7134 1544 4

Filmset in 'Monophoto' Plantin by
Servis Filmsetting Limited, Manchester

Printed in Great Britain by

The Anchor Press Limited, Tiptree, Essex
for the publishers
B T Batsford Limited, 4 Fitzhardinge Street, London W1H 0AH

Contents

Acknowledgment

The Author wishes to acknowledge the generous help provided by many institutions and individuals, including a number of manufacturers of screenprinting equipment and materials.

Introduction

The process described in this book is a method of printing which is traditionally referred to as silk screen printing, although nowadays the term *serigraphy* is applied to the medium, particularly when it is used for the production of fine art prints.

As a process of graphic reproduction, screen printing is unique in so much as it requires very little by way of sophisticated equipment but as a medium in the hands of the experienced printer can rival photo-lithography in the scope and quality of the work that can be achieved.

Screen printing is in essence a form of stencilling first used by the Chinese many centuries ago but which was largely unknown in the West until the middle of this century. It has since become one of the most widely used and versatile of all reprographic processes, being employed in virtually every area of printing from the production of high quality fabrics and wallpapers, to the lettering on plastic detergent bottles; from pictures on tee shirts to full colour posters and artists prints.

The aim of this book is to provide the reader with an introduction to the technique of screen printing, to offer advice on the purchase and construction of the necessary equipment – much of which can, in fact, be made or improvised in the studio or home workshop and to suggest a range of experiments which will form a basis for the use of the medium as a means of creative expression.

Of necessity in a book of this kind less consideration will be given to the more 'commercial' aspects of the subject. But since in even the most sophisticated industrial screen printing plants, the equipment is often very little different from that used by the individual artist in his studio, the reader will not find it difficult to adapt his understanding of the medium to more commercial ends should his interests develop in that direction.

A letter O in a conventional stencil showing ‘tie bars’ holding the centre in place

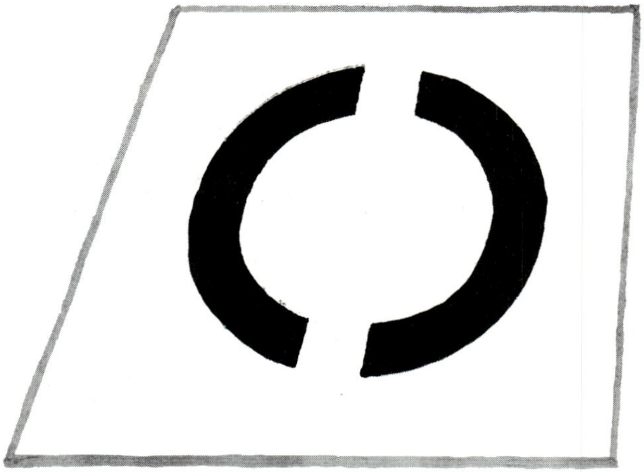

A screen printed O showing the mesh of the material holding the centre in place

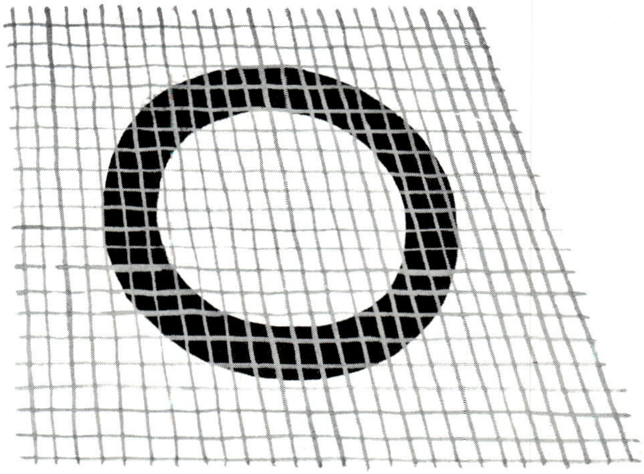

The basic principle

A printing screen consists simply of a rectangular frame over which some loosely woven material (traditionally silk but now more commonly a cotton or man-made fibre) is stretched, making what is in effect a very fine sieve. The material is 'blocked out' wherever the designer requires the image to remain white or unprinted, and colouring matter is then brushed or squeegeed through the mesh of the material.

In other words screen printing is simply a form of stencilling where the warp and weft of a material is used to hold the pieces of the stencil in place, thereby obviating the need for 'ties' between one area of stencil and the next.

Almost any substance that can be painted or glued to the material and which will not dissolve or become detached in the printing medium will serve to block out the screen provided that it does not add appreciably to the overall thickness of the material.

It has already been suggested that screen printing is capable of producing highly sophisticated results, particularly when combined with photographic techniques, and some of these processes will be fully described later in this book. However, the basic principle is so simple that the beginner needs very little experience of the medium before he can start to invent and improvise techniques for himself.

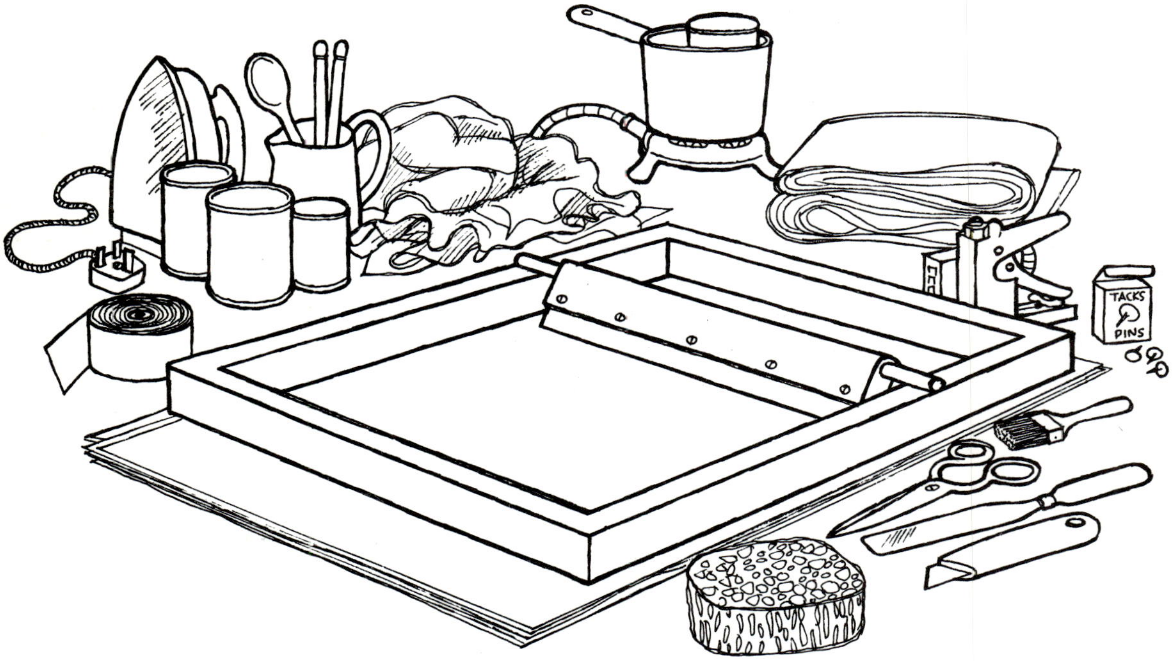

The basic equipment required to begin the preliminary experiments in screen printing:- including screen, squeegee, newsprint, spoons, flat iron, cans and pots, rag, sponge, scissors, paint brushes, adhesive tape and gum strip, staple gun or thumb tacks, boiling ring and saucepans, screen mesh, palette knives, sharp trimming knife

Equipment and materials

For the beginner there are only really two special items of equipment that are needed over and above the kind of equipment that is generally found in an artist's studio or school classroom, the screen itself and the squeegee.

Access to a sink with running hot and cold water is helpful, and if one is in the fortunate position of being able to set up a studio especially for screen printing then the installation of a screen-washing sink of the kind described on page 22 will prove a great advantage.

The facility for melting and dissolving a range of substances will be needed and this can be supplied by any form of heating ring, even a camping stove if a main gas or electricity supply is not available.

For the first experiments in screen printing a specialised printing table is not required. Any large, flat topped table will do provided it can be washed down easily – laminated plastic is ideal. For more advanced work, including fabric printing, more sophisticated printing surfaces may be required and these are available from specialist suppliers or can be put together on a do-it-yourself basis as described on page 71.

Other items of a more general nature include:
Spoons, bowls, jam and other storage jars, scissors, tin cans, sponges, paint brushes, plastic cartons, staple gun, thumb tacks, palette knives, measuring jar, domestic flat-iron, soldering iron, old kitchen knives, rag, adhesive tape and gumstrip, old newspapers, etc, etc.

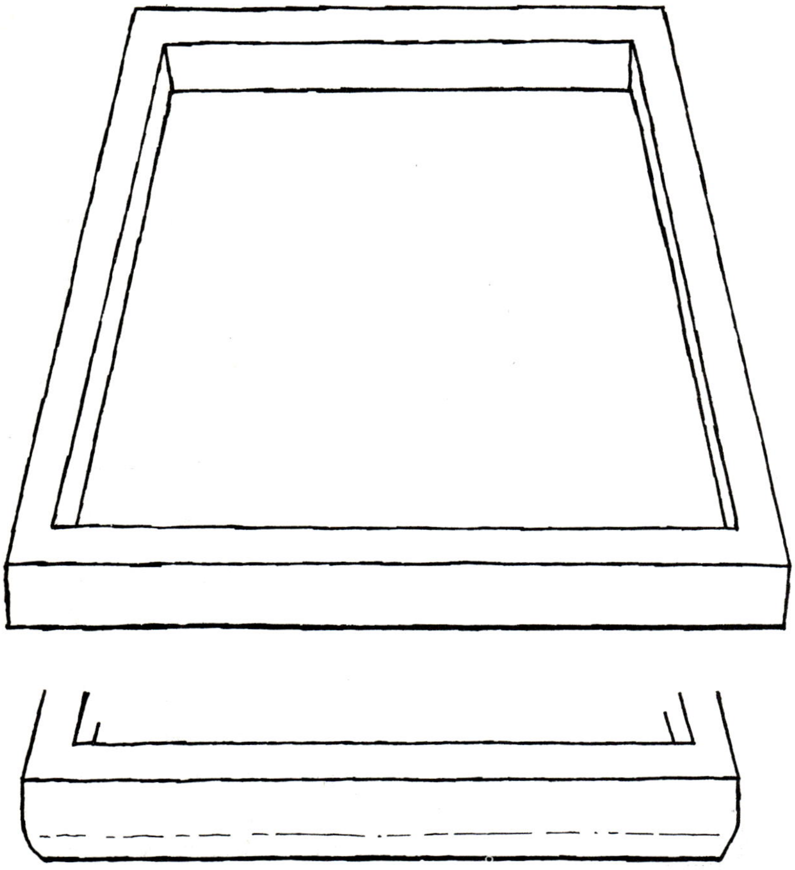

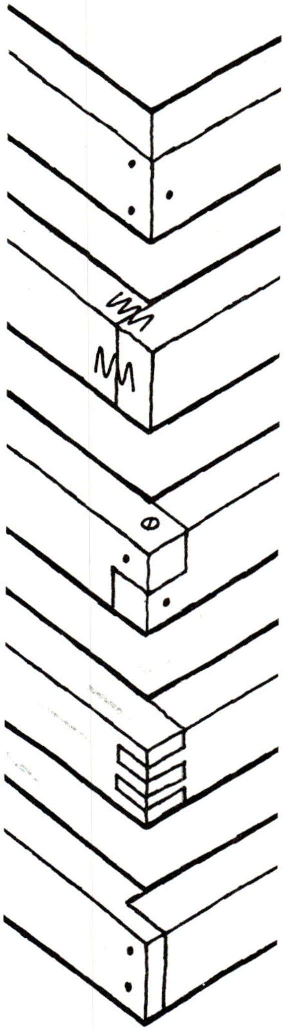

Basic wooden screen frame and 5 methods of jointing the corners
1 Mitre-pinned and glued. Although a mitre is not generally considered a very sound joint, when cut on a first class mitre-cutting machine it works quite well
2 Butt joint fixed with corrugated dogs
3 Halving joint pinned, glued and screwed
4 Combed joint, very professional if one has access to a suitable woodworking machine. One could also use a simple dovetail
5 Shoulder joint pinned and glued
It is advisable to use waterproof glue and non-ferrous pins and screws for all joints

The screen frame

The printing screen consists of a simple rectangular frame generally made from a timber which is soft enough to accept drawing pins or staples, and yet firm enough to withstand the considerable stresses put upon it in the course of stretching the mesh and its subsequent use in the printing process. Since most screens are repeatedly washed in water the timber used should also be of a kind unlikely to warp or rot. The best professional frames are generally constructed from cedar wood which is noted for its stability in damp conditions. It is possible to improvise screen frames from old pictures frames but far too often these are made from oak or some other form of hardwood, to which it is difficult to fix the mesh.

However, assuming the availability of a supply of good quality, knot-free timber, screen frames can be put together quite easily and cheaply by the printmaker himself. There are several methods for constructing a screen, depending on the carpentry skill available. The choice of the size of timber to be used is important and it pays to use a section which is of a larger dimension than is absolutely necessary, it does not pay to skimp. The use of a heavier timber does not only make for a more stable frame but makes the jointing of the corners much easier. For sizes of frame up to about one metre square, a 6 × 4 cm section is about right.

Jointing the corners does not provide any real difficulties, provided one uses a combination of waterproof glue and nails or screws (oval nails are best as there is less tendency to split the wood). Methods suitable for jointing the corners are shown on page 12. The use of a mitre-cramp to hold the joint in place whilst it is being fixed can be recommended although it is not essential. Corrugated fasteners can also be used to advantage to provide extra rigidity but hammering them into place does require a little experience.

When the screen is complete it is advisable to rub the corners down with glasspaper which will make the stretching of the mesh easier to do. Some professionally produced screen frames are bevelled in such a way that only a narrow section of the frame actually makes contact with the printing surface (see page 12).

The experienced printer will need to have a wide range of screen sizes available to him, but for the beginner it is advisable to make or purchase screens of the same size, chosen to relate in size to the width of the mesh material it is intended to use. All

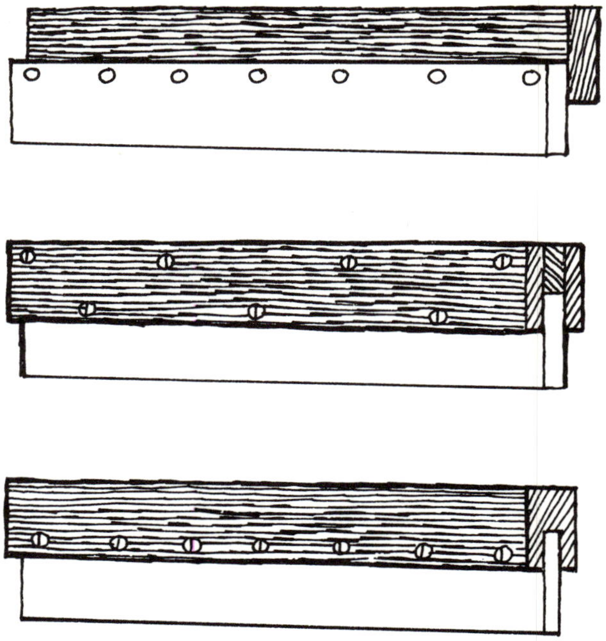

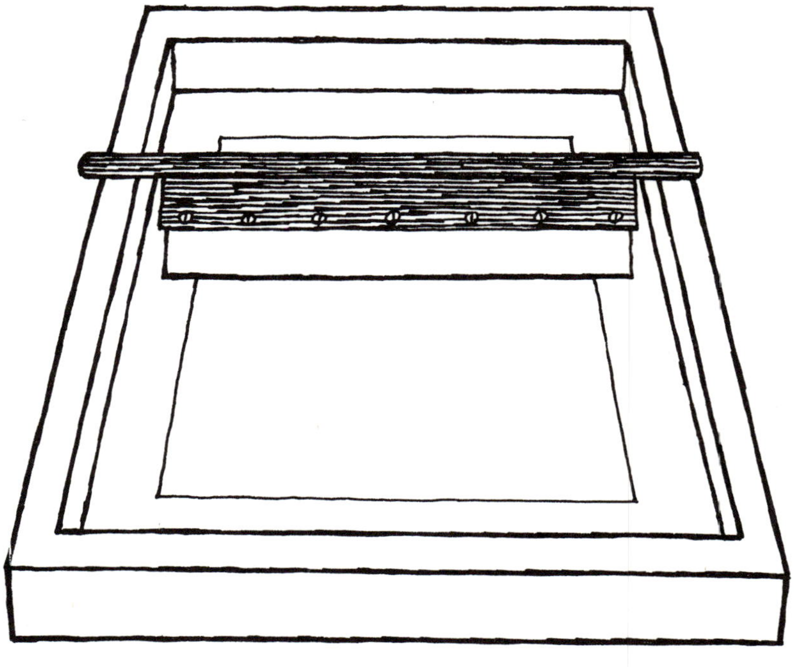

Three methods of construction of a squeegee. Waterproof glues should always be used together with non-ferrous screws or nails. To prevent the squeegee from slipping into the pigment a strip of wood can be fixed along the back of the squeegee handle screen mesh materials are becoming increasingly expensive and for the sake of economy one must try to avoid cutting the material to waste. One should aim to cut *exactly* one, two, three or whatever number of screens from a particular width of material.

Another advantage of standardising one's screens is that if this is done, it is also possible to standardise one's squeegees so that there is never any doubt that any squeegee will fit the screen.

In deciding on the size of screen most suited to one's purposes, it must be remembered that the 'masked out' area occupies a considerable part of the total area of the screen and that if there is to be a reasonable part of the screen remaining to form the image, the overall dimensions of the screen must be larger than one would at first imagine. Unless the reader intends to concentrate on producing images the size of postcards, it is unwise to invest in screen frames which are less than 40 cm in their smallest dimension.

Squeegees

The ink or dye in which the design is to be printed can, in practice, be brushed through the screen with a decorator's brush or rubbed through with a sponge or cloth. But for quickness and in order to obtain an even spread of pigment, it is necessary to use a squeegee.

A squeegee generally consists of a flat blade of hard rubber or polyurethane plastic, set into a wooden handle. It is not too difficult to make or improvise squeegees, provided it is recognised that the blade must be straight and the edge undamaged. In the absence of the recognised rubber or plastic material it is even possible to improvise a blade using hardboard of masonite. A hardboard blade works quite well so long as it is the manufacturer's edge that is used or if one is forced to use a sawn edge, this must be planed absolutely straight. It also helps to rub down the sharp corners of the blade with a fine glasspaper.

Various ways of making a squeegee are illustrated on page 14. Squeegee rubber or compound is sold by the metre length in soft, medium or hard grades. 47 × 9 mm is the standard section but other dimensions are available. The choice of grade is to some extent dependent on the kind of work to be done and upon the particular preferences of the user. My recommendation would be for the reader to opt for a harder rather than a softer grade of material. Black squeegee rubber should be avoided, particularly if it is intended to print in spirit based inks.

What is required of a squeegee is that it should force a thin even film of pigment through the stencil and for this purpose I find a blade with a square section the most useful. Some professionaly manufactured squeegees have the working edge of the blade cut to a V-section, like the blade of a knife. I can see no particular advantage in this and I would certainly not recommend the reader to try to shape his own squeegee blades in this fashion.

It is a considerable advantage to have a projection at each end of the squeegee handle which is long enough to overhang the screen frame and prevent the squeegee falling into the pigment thus allowing the printer to leave the squeegee in the screen throughout the printing process. It is advisable to use a squeegee which is approximately 5 cm (2 in.) shorter than the inside dimension of the screen, this will permit easy movement from one end of the screen to the other.

Care of squeegees

The success of any screen printing operation depends more than anything else on the serviceability of the squeegee. It is therefore very important to look after squeegees most carefully. They should be cleaned thoroughly after each period of use and stored in such a way that there is no chance of the blades becoming indented as a result of squeegees resting one upon another. It is also unwise to store squeegees in very warm conditions – a cupboard beside a radiator for example. In the long term, it is advisable to construct a rack in which this vital item of equipment can be stored in safety.

Pigments

Screen printing techniques can be used to apply a very wide range of colouring substances to an equally wide variety of materials. The application of screen printing to printed ephemera, posters, etc and to the production of fabrics and wallpapers has been extended to include a whole new range of modern applications including printed electrical circuitry, plastic packaging and the like. Each of these specialist applications demand a particular type of ink or dye, and these are discussed in the section on inks (see page 18).

For his first experiments in screen printing the reader will require only the most basic of colouring materials. All paints, inks and dyes consist of the colouring agent or pigment and the liquid in which the pigment is dissolved or suspended. Sometimes this liquid is made up of a number of different ingredients and sometimes yet another liquid substance is used as a diluent or solvent. Although it is not a strictly scientific use of the term, *pigment* will be used throughout this book to describe any colouring material that is squeegeed through the mesh of the screen.

In practice almost any kind of pigment can be used with a screen provided that:

(*a*) it is of the correct consistency, ie not so this that it will spread or run under the blocked areas of the stencil, or so thick or lumpy that it will not pass through the mesh.

(*b*) it will not dry so quickly that the screen cannot be left for a few moments without the mesh becoming blocked.

(*c*) it is suitable for the surface on to which it is being printed and it will dry to a reasonably permanent state.

From the screen printer's point of view there are basically two kinds of colouring materials. One, which we generally refer to as *paints or inks*, the other as *dyes*. In practice the situation is somewhat confused. For example a pigment which is designed to be printed onto cloth is almost always called a dye, although many such substances are actually paints or inks.

Perhaps the position can be best explained in the following way:

A paint or ink consists of a pigmenting material which is finely ground into a powder and suspended in a medium which when it is dry binds the particles of pigment together and to the surface on which the material is laid.

A dye consists of a pigmenting material in solution which reacts with the fabric onto which it has been printed in such a way that when it has been fixed by heat or some other kind of treatment it becomes an integral part of the fabric.

Under the first heading we can include the kind of pigment, not strictly designed for screen printing, which is generally available in an art studio; pigments such as tempera or poster colour, all of which are water-based.

Most paints of this kind can be used for screen printing, either directly or with the addition of extenders. Many paint manufacturers supply *extenders* designed to make the paint more suitable as a screen printing medium, particularly in schools and colleges. Any paint used for screen printing must be thoroughly mixed to ensure that there are no lumps to block the screen and that the pigment is well dispersed throughout the medium. Coagulated particles of pigment become trapped under the squeegee blade, causing streaks in the flat, coloured areas of the print.

Most paints of the kind described above are extremely opaque and do not permit the printer to obtain the overprinting effects which can be such an exciting aspect of any printing process. A really economic printing medium can be produced by adding domestic dye powder to a cellulose wallpaper paste. This medium is very transparent and provided each successive colour is allowed to dry completely before printing the next, some very satisfactory results can be obtained. It is advisable to mix the paste a little thicker than is usually suggested in the instructions and the dye must be thoroughly dissolved in a little warm water before it is added to the paste. One disadvantage of this pigment is its tendency to stain hands and clothing so from that point of view care must be exercised in its use. Although the pigment is a fabric dye, used in the mixture described above it would not be suitable for fabric printing if a permanent result is desired.

It has already been pointed out that a vast range of specialised pigments are now available to the screen printer and these are described in some detail in the next section of the book. However it is suggested that the beginner experiments with one or two of the more basic pigments before investing in more sophisticated and expensive materials.

Inks

The increasing popularity of screen printing as a commercial and industrial medium has encouraged the pigment manufacturers to produce a bewildering range of different inks, bewildering that is to the beginner. Each ink is designed for a specific purpose and is matched to a particular process or printing surface. Fortunately most of these inks will be of no immediate interest to the reader of this book. When he does reach the stage in the development of his screen printing craft when it is necessary to become more knowledgeable in these matters, he will find that most manufacturers of screen process supplies provide very detailed information sheets about the use of their products.

In general terms all inks can be divided into three main categories:

1 Inks which are based on a PVA or other plastic medium and used in conjunction with water, both as a thinner and as a washing-out agent.

2 Inks which are oil-based and require mineral or white spirit as a thinner and as a washing-out agent. In practice, many commercially produced inks of this kind prove difficult to remove from the screen at the completion of the printing run and require the use of an enhanced spirit or screen cleaner. This screen cleaner is a very powerful solvent and should only be handled whilst wearing protective gloves.

3 Inks which are cellulose-based and require cellulose thinners and cleaners. Although it is necessary to mention these inks they are not recommended for use by any but the most experienced printer.

Each product is supplied with manufacturers' instructions as to suitable thinners, drying time etc. The main point to remember is to mix the ink thoroughly to a consistency which flows well under the pressure of the squeegee. Some inks are *self solvent*, ie they can be left in the screen for short periods of time and can be reactivated by one or two sweeps of the squeegee when re-commencing work. It is important to remember that when working in a warm room, inks will gradually thicken as the medium evaporates and should be re-mixed from time to time with fresh thinner.

Most inks have an indefinite shelf life, provided that they are stored in airtight containers, and care should be taken to ensure that a skin does not form on top of the ink. Should the ink skin over, it must be carefully strained before further use, since even the smallest fragment of hard ink will be forced by the squeegee into the mesh, causing a block in the print.

Most screen printing inks are opaque, each subsequent printed colour completely obliterating its predecessor. However, it is possible to obtain a material called a *transparent base*, with which the inks can be mixed, rendering them more or less transparent, depending on how great a proportion of base is used. In this way some very exciting overprinting effects can be obtained. When overprinting in transparent colours it is generally advisable to begin with the lightest colour and progress to the darkest. In this way the widest range of secondary and tertiary coloured effects can be obtained.

Opaque inks can be printed on virtually any colour or type of paper. However, unless one chooses a tinted or coloured paper for a particular reason the best results are obtained by printing on really white cartridge paper; this is especially true when using a transparent pigment. The actual surface characteristics of the paper are not as critical in screen printing as they would be in many other forms of printing and because of the flexibility of the mesh it is possible to make a screen print onto a moderately textured surface. At the end of each printing session, it is necessary to clean the screen thoroughly. With water-based pigments this does not generally present too many problems. The screen is simply placed on a flat surface, preferably not the one used to print on, and after removing as much pigment as possible with a spoon or palette knife (this can be returned to the pot) the screen is sponged out with a damp sponge. Finally it is stood on end and two nearly dry sponges are used in conjunction, one from each side, to remove the last vestiges of the pigment.

Oil-based inks can be removed in a similar way except that rags and white spirit are used instead of sponges and water. However most modern oil-based inks are only moderately soluble in normal white or mineral spirit and the last part of the process, where the screen is stood on its end, requires the use of the special screen cleaner supplied for this purpose.

If a screen should become caked with dried ink it can generally be restored with the aid of decorator's paint stripper, but this is an operation which is best avoided by careful management.

After cleaning, a screen mesh should be examined against a light to ensure no traces of pigment or cleaner remain and then the screen is ready for the next printing session.

It is important to clean the screen thoroughly in the manner described before attempting to remove a stencil by whatever method is appropriate to that particular stencil. When the screen has been stripped the mesh should be re-scoured with a strong detergent or a screen de-greasing agent.

The mesh

By far the most important component of a printing screen is the mesh which supports the stencil and through which the pigment is squeegeed. The original material was silk, and the whole process is sometimes still referred to as silk screen printing. Silk has never been a cheap material – certainly not in the west – and the cost of silk is now so prohibitive that its use is now out of the question except for work which is on a very small scale or of a very specialised nature.

Cotton took the place of silk and although it has none of the fineness or strength of silk it was reasonably cheap and generally fairly serviceable for normal requirements. However the development of man-made fibres, coupled with the increasing cost and deteriorating quality of cotton organdies, has brought about a situation in which man-made fibres based on polymide or polyester are used almost exclusively for screen meshes.

Cotton still possesses one advantage over the man-made materials. It is not very elastic and can easily be stretched over the screen frame by hand. It also shrinks when wet so that even an indifferently stretched mesh will often shrink into shape after the screen has been washed for the first time. However cotton is not very durable, can be easily torn – particularly when being stretched – and soon begins to sag.

Man-made fibres, nylon and terylene, to use the names commonly applied to them, are made up into screen mesh materials in a number of ways, each one suited to a particular range of requirements.

Monofilament terylenes are manufactured from single filament yarns and are rapidly gaining acceptance as the best materials for general use. The original monofilaments, because of their construction, lacked 'tooth' and were not always very suitable for use with adhesive stencils, although this problem is now being overcome.

Multifilament terylenes are made up by spinning together a number of single threads and in that sense are closer to natural fabrics. Because of this form of construction, multifilament fabrics accept the stencil more readily but do not have the micromesh regularity of the monofilament materials – a factor which is not something about which the beginner has need to concern himself.

Monofilament nylons are more elastic than monofilament terylenes and are therefore more suited to printing on ceramic and other irregular shaped objects.

The other factor to consider when choosing a mesh fabric is its fineness or coarseness, usually measured in terms of threads to the inch or centimetre. Meshes are available ranging from about 30 threads to the centimetre (about 80 threads to the inch) to over 120 to the centimetre (300 to the inch). The very fine

A palette knife that has been filed square at the end is a most useful tool for removing pigment from the screen. The corners should not be sharp for fear of damaging the mesh. In the absence of a large palette knife an old kitchen knife, treated in the same way, will work almost as well

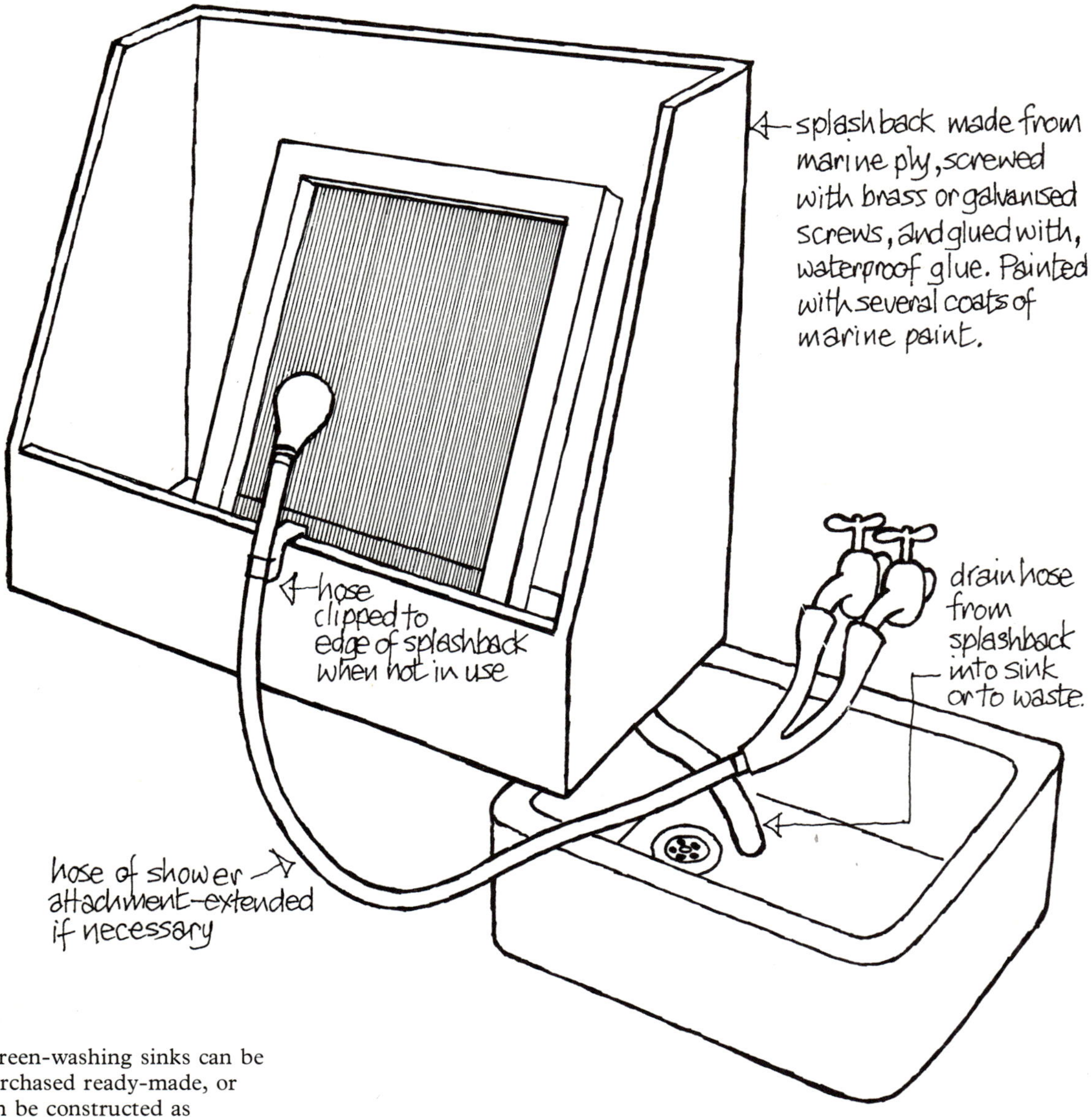

Screen-washing sinks can be purchased ready-made, or can be constructed as indicated in this drawing. 15 mm marine ply should be used if possible and as an extra precaution against leaks, all joints could be reinforced with fibreglass and resin. When a sink with running water is not available, the waste can be extended to run to the nearest drain, and the water supplied from a garden watering-can meshes are designed for specialised work involving the reproduction of half-tone photographs. For the artist screenprinter a mesh of around 20 to 24 threads to the centimetre (100 to 120 threads to the inch) is generally satisfactory.

The characteristic of a screen mesh is the equal distribution of warp and weft threads producing a material in which the spaces between the fibres are exactly square. It is possible to make screens using domestic terylene curtaining fabrics which can often be purchased quite cheaply from a local draper. However when doing so, it is advisable to take a magnifying glass along the check the character of the weave. Some domestic organdies are constructed with fancy meshes which make the material more elastic in one direction than the other. Needless to say it is quite impossible to stretch a drum-tight screen with such a material.

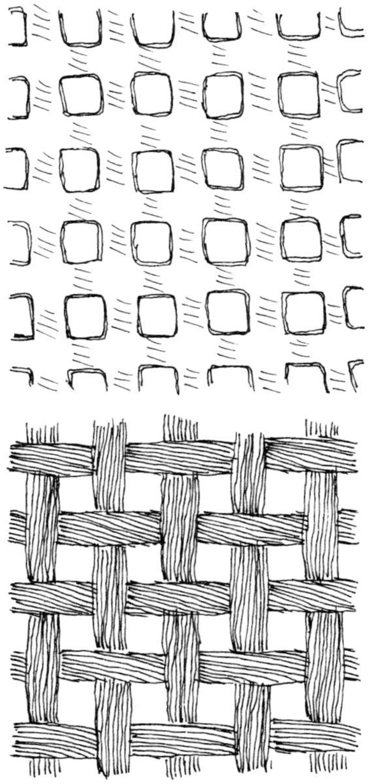

Enlargements of mesh structure. Monofilament polyester mesh (above) and (below) multifilament polyester mesh

Stretching the mesh

Covering the screen frame with the mesh is one of the most important stages in the craft of screen printing. The mesh should be drum-tight, the tension being equal in all directions. This is fairly easily achieved when using cotton organdie, partly because, as has already been mentioned, the cotton will shrink into shape when it has been made wet. Hand stretching man-made fibres is more difficult, and for the kind of perfect results needed for the most sophisticated work it is advisable to make use of a stretching machine or to employ the services of a professional screen-stretching agency. Very few of the processes described in this book require that the screen be stretched to perfection and if the procedures described on page 24 are followed, satisfactory results should be obtained.

Great care must be taken when stretching cotton by hand as many modern cotton organdies do not stand up to excessive or uneven tension and will tear suddenly and dramatically in the middle of the stretching process.

On the other hand, man-made fibres seem to be almost indestructible and should be stretched under the maximum tension available. Drawing pins (thumb tacks) or staples can be used to hold the mesh to the frame, and whenever possible an appropriate, waterproof glue should also be used to supplement the pins or tacks.

Before any work is done on the stretched screen the mesh must be thoroughly scoured or de-greased to remove 'dress' or other impurities. Screen printing suppliers market de-greasing

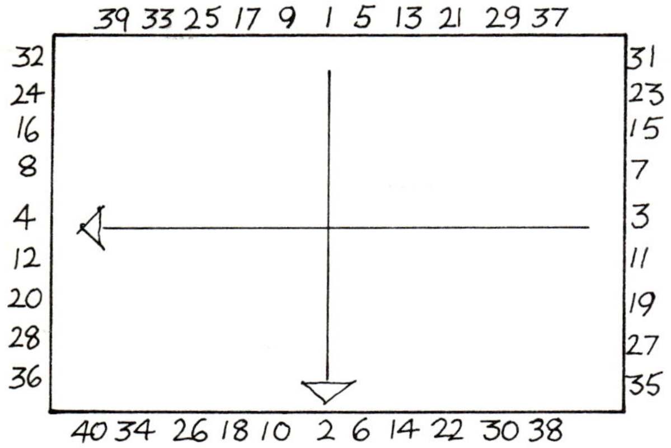

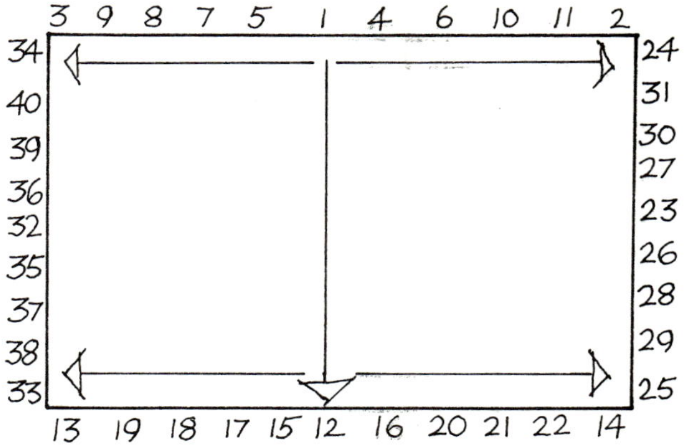

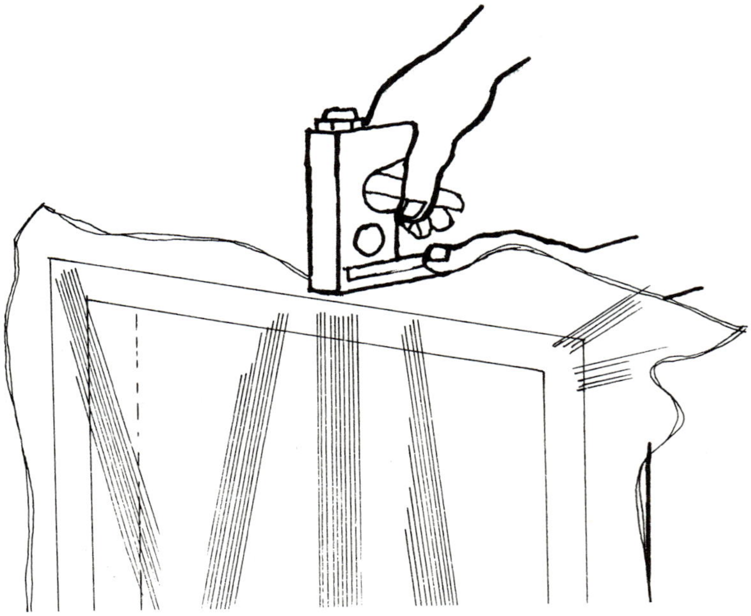

Two methods of stretching the mesh by hand; numbers represent the order in which staples are inserted. Maximum possible tension should be applied at all times and particular care taken to make sure that the mesh is really taut at the corners. It helps to work with the edge of the screen being stapled held at waist level, which probably means working with the bottom edge of the screen on the seat of a chair and not on a table top. If the staples are inserted through a strip of card, they are easier to remove when the screen needs to be re-stretched, but holding the card in place while stretching the mesh can be quite a difficult operation for the beginner. Nylon or polyester meshes are difficult to stretch by hand and in order to obtain maximum tension it is necessary to use canvas-straining pliers

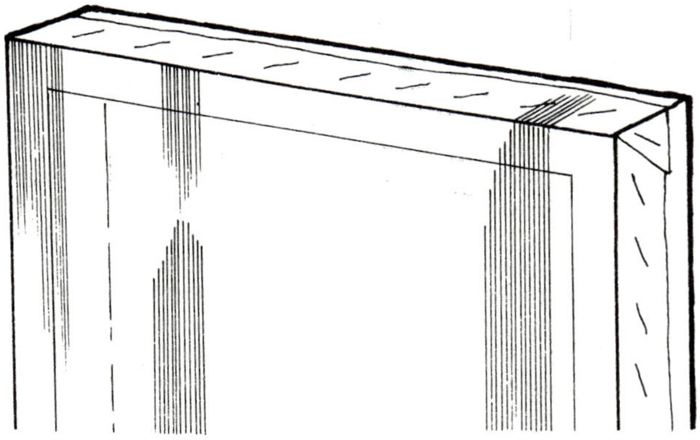

agents, but in most cases a good scrub using a strong detergent liquid will suffice. Some screen printers advocate scouring a terylene mesh with scouring powder as this is reputed to give a little more tooth to the fabric. If this practice is followed, however, it is most important that the mesh is very thoroughly washed afterwards to remove all traces of the powder. Scouring powder should never be used on a cotton fabric as it will cause felting.

A well-stretched screen will have the warp of the mesh running parallel to the screen frame. With this in mind it is always advisable to commence the stretching process by fixing a selvedge of the material to the screen first. If no selvedge is available an edge should be created by cutting or tearing along the line of the warp or weft.

Masking

Before the screen can be used for printing it will need to be masked so that only a rectangle of mesh, the overall shape and size of the design to be printed, remains open in the centre of the screen. The border formed in this way will not only serve to control the shape of the printed area, but will also act as a reservoir for the pigment. The most usual way to create this masked area is by the use of gummed paper strip (5 cm (2 in.) wide is the most suitable). The strips are stuck directly on to the mesh on the outside of the screen, as shown in the illustration on page 28, and should overlap each other by about 1 cm ($\frac{1}{4}$ in.). The outside strip should be taken up to the outside of the screen frame, to prevent any possibility of the pigment seeping out of the frame on to the border of the print.

The secret of getting the gumstrip to adhere firmly to the mesh lies in making sure that it is thoroughly soaked before it is applied. A wringing wet sponge can be used to wet the strip or better still, the length of gumstrip can actually be run through a bowl of water or under a running tap. Rubbing the strip with a sponge that is not really wet only succeeds in removing the gum.

Whether or not one masks the screen before putting the stencil on to it, depends to some extent on the kind of stencil to be used. For example, if a photographic technique is to be employed which will necessitate the total washing out of the screen with warm water, then any gumstrip previously applied, will, of course, be washed away and valuable time will be wasted. Many coating emulsions will, in practice, provide a fairly substantial masked area and this will only require touching-up or making-ready before the printing process can commence.

In some of the early experiments or in instances where long printing runs are not required, it is possible to work with only the outside of the screen frame masked. But in order to prevent pigment seeping into the space between the mesh and the frame it is necessary to mask the inside of the frame also. This operation is a little more difficult, and care must be taken to

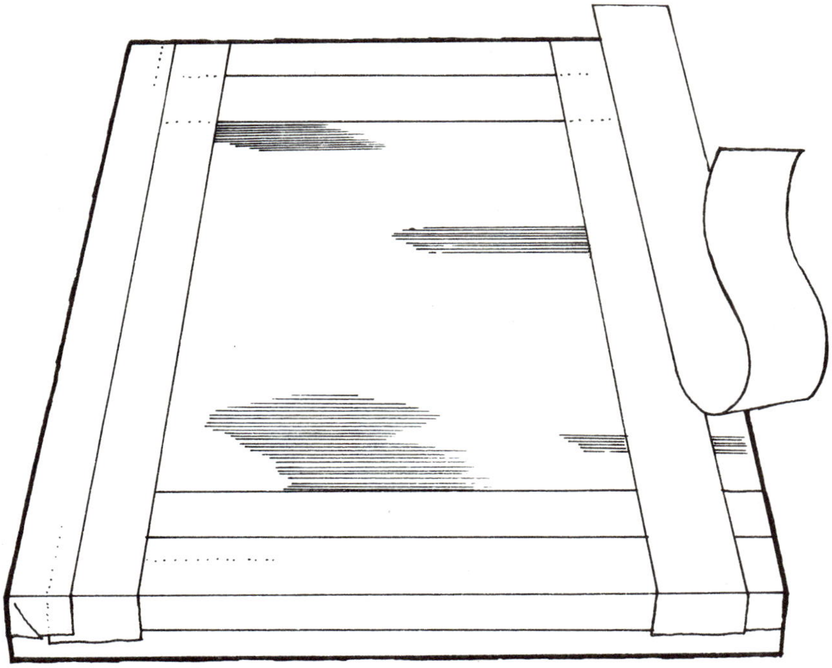

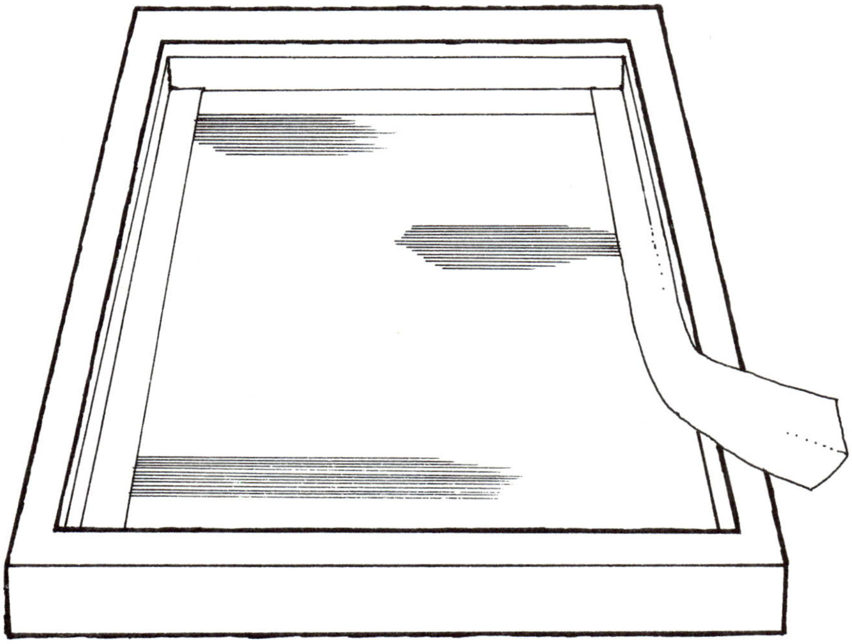

Gummed paper strip is used to mask both the inside and the outside edges of the screen, and to control the printing area of the stencil. It is advisable to cut all the strips to length before gumming them in place. In this way one can avoid any possibility of getting water on to the roll of gumstrip ensure that no lumps and bumps are created which will interfere with the passage of the squeegee.

When printing in water-based pigments one would imagine that there is a danger of the gumstrip becoming loosened by the dye. In practice this rarely seems to happen; more often than not the pigment builds up behind the gumstrip so that even when the strip is removed that area of the screen remains blocked with solid dye. However, to be on the safe side, when using a screen for a long printing run with water-based pigments, it is as well to seal the inside mask with a coating of waterproof varnish.

One final word of warning: always allow the gumstrip to dry with the screen in a horizontal position. If a screen is propped against a wall to dry liquid gum will dribble down from under the strip and block the screen. If this does happen the gum can be removed with warm water but sometimes it is not noticed until the stencil is in place.

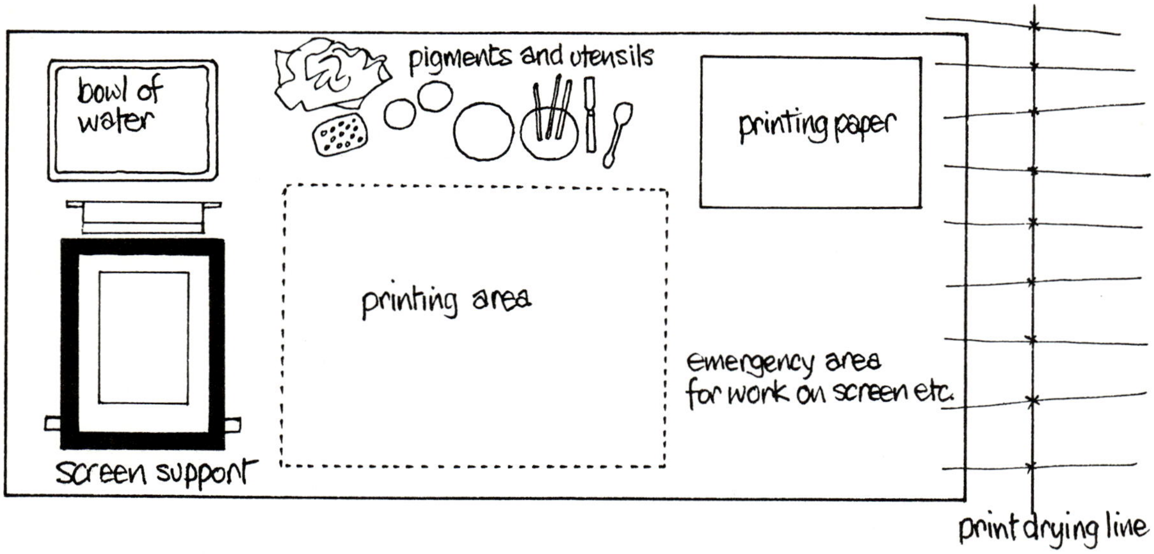

Very basic arrangement for the beginner using water based pigment

The organisation of the printing area

As with most crafts, the screen printer will begin to work in a fairly simple way and his initial requirements in terms of accommodation and equipment will be relatively modest, gradually becoming more sophisticated as his skills and interests develop. Nevertheless, from the outset it is most important that the area in which the printing is to take place is carefully planned and arranged. It is all too easy to find oneself with a screen full of wet pigment in one's hands, and surrounded by wet prints with nowhere to put anything down.

The basic requirements of the printing area are as follows:

1 A flat table with sufficient space to support the screen when in use, the screen at rest, printing paper, pigments, solvents, brushes, sponges, cleaning rags, squeegees etc. An arrangement similar to the one indicated on page 30 works quite well.

2 Support for the drying prints in the form of a hanging rack or drying shelves.

It will be seen that the above is indeed very basic, the sort of set-up that could be created even in the corner of one's bedroom. But the establishment of a screen workshop is an organic process; items of equipment are added and procedures modified as experience is gained. A studio layout is a very personal affair and the reader will have no great difficulty in developing his own arrangement as his craft develops. The ultimate arrangement will include a vacuum table, tracing table, washing sink, light box (for the exposure of photo-sensitive stencils) even dark-room facilities; but for the first experiments, a pad of newspapers opened out on a table, so that the area is large enough to take the size of the screen, will serve as a printing surface; a bowl of water, a sink; and the sunlight shining through the window, the light box. A printing surface consisting of a pad of newspapers has many advantages since each successive sheet can be removed and destroyed as it becomes soiled with pigment. Cleanliness is a problem in screen printing since one is dealing with a fairly fluid pigment used over a large printing area (compared with other print-making processes such as

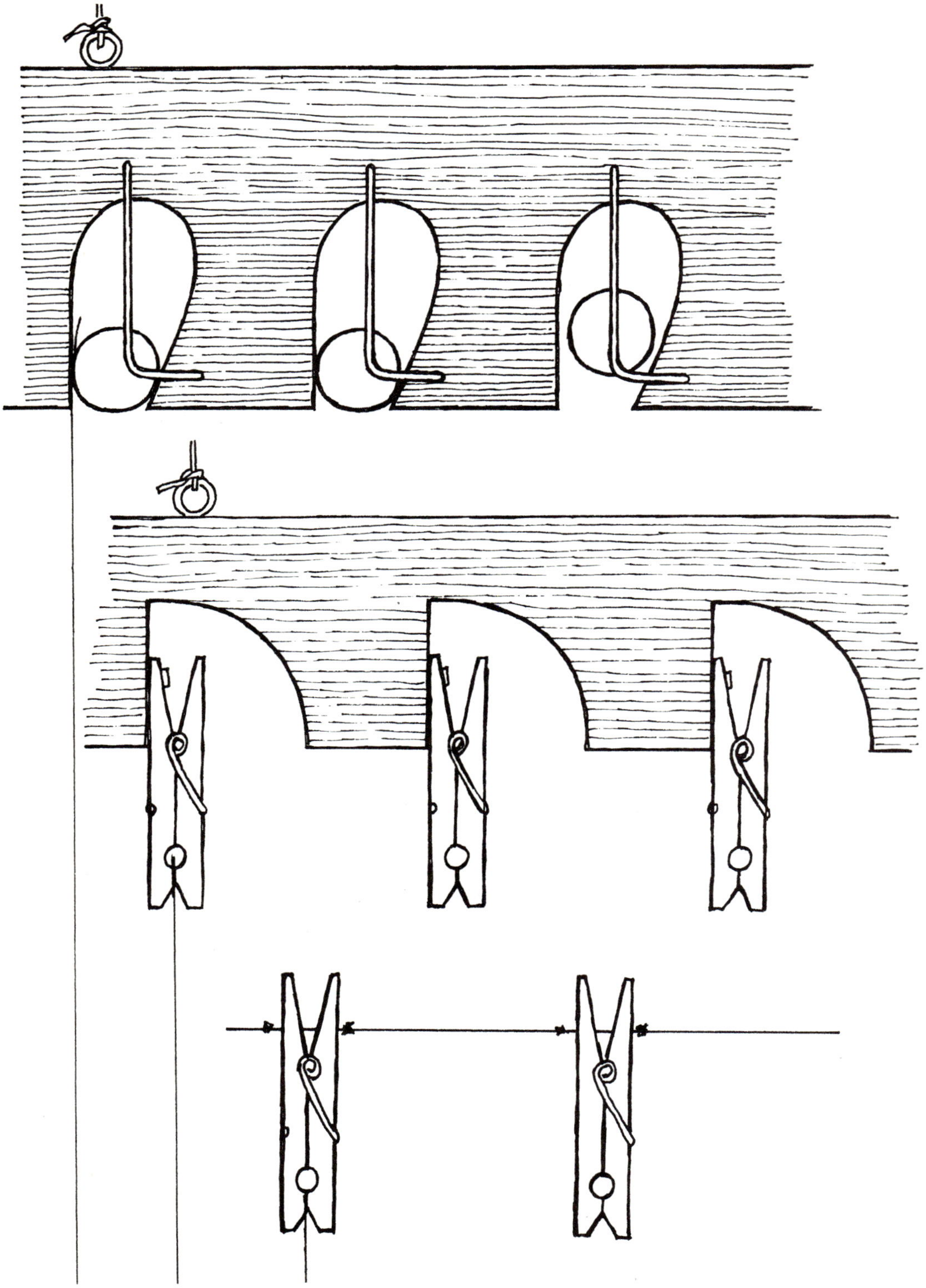

blockprinting, etching, lithography etc). It is certainly an advantage to work on a table that can be cleaned down easily, one with a laminate surface for example.

When printing with a screen which is held in the hand, as distinct from one which is clamped to a printing table, space must be provided to accommodate the screen between prints and one end of the screen must always be supported an inch or so above the table top by means of a slat of wood to prevent the wet mesh from sticking to the table. Supporting the screen at a slight angle also ensures that the pigment is retained against the bottom of the frame and does not creep over the stencil area.

Opposite Three of the many systems available for the suspension of drying prints
1 A commercially manufactured ball and patten rack. The ball is held in place by the wire (sometimes a metal plate) and falls against the paper holding it tight to the wood
2 A home made rack; shapes are cut from a length of 75 mm × 50 mm (3 in. × 2 in.) timber with a jig-saw and the pegs are glued and or nailed into place. It is advisable to drill the pegs before nailing
3 Probably the simplest system of all. Clothes pegs are drilled and strung on a line
With all these systems it is important to allow sufficient distance between each peg, particularly if large prints are to be produced. It is possible to rack prints horizontally and units are manufactured which work in this way. However, since studio floor space is nearly always at a premium it is generally more sensible to make use of the space above one's head by using racks which can be hoisted up out of the way

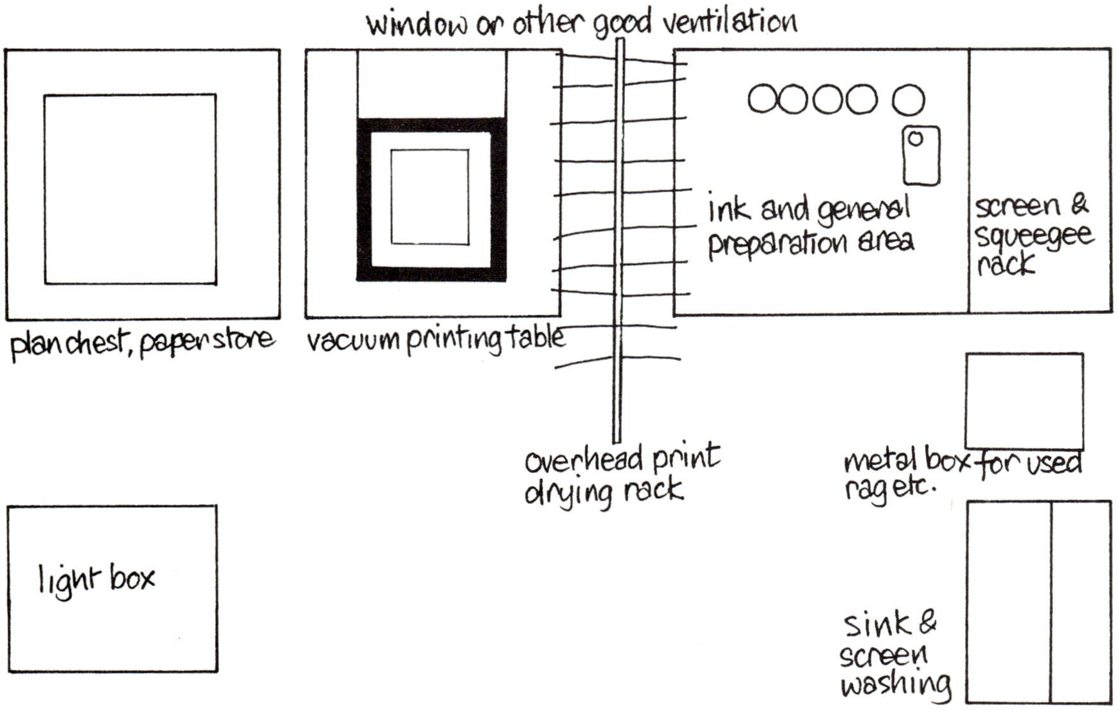

More sophisticated printmaking set-up for use with oil, inks etc.

It is virtually impossible to describe the ideal studio layout for the more sophisticated printmaker. So much will depend on the amount of accommodation available and the financial resources at the disposal of the printmaker.

The diagram above sets out, in schematic fashion, the kind of provision that would be a minimum requirement for the artist intending to produce prints on a professional basis. The choice and positioning of a print drying rack is very much a matter of personal preference but should not be located too far from the vacuum table.

Other matters to be taken into consideration include the storage of materials; always remembering that inflammable liquids should be kept in a fireproof container, dark room provision if much photographic imagery is to be employed and ventilation. Not only is good ventilation important from the health and safety point of view but the atmospheric conditions in a studio can affect the quality of the printmaking itself, eg the stability of paper and stencils and the drying time of the completed prints.

Using the squeegee

Apart from the designing and general graphic techniques needed to enable an image to be produced on the screen, the only specific skill required by the screen printer is the ability to manipulate the squeegee; and after a little practice with a plain screen and some gum or even water, this technique can soon be mastered. The aim is to force a thin, even film of pigment through the mesh. If the squeegee is held too lightly or at the wrong angle, the film of pigment will be too thick, leaving an indistinct image on the paper or fabric. Considerable pressure is also needed to force the stencil down hard against the surface to be printed thus preventing pigment from seeping into the areas which it is intended should remain clear (see illustration page 36).

The best prints are produced when the mesh is held a few millimetres above the surface to be printed until the moment when the squeegee blade actually passes. This is referred to as *snap distance* but it can only be achieved when the paper is held down by a vacuum or, in the case of fabric printing, when the fabric is gummed down to the table.

The masking strips at each end of the screen act as reservoirs for the pigment and before the first print is taken the printer must ensure that sufficient pigment is spread evenly along the masking strip furthest away from him. The exact amount of pigment required for a particular pull will depend on the character of the stencil, ie whether or not there are large open areas demanding large quantities of pigment. It is a great mistake to try to print with too little pigment for to run out in the middle of a pull almost invariably results in a spoilt print. This is particularly true when printing in transparent inks on paper or in dyes on fabric. This is one reason why it is a mistake to make the masked border too narrow. A generous border area will accommodate a good supply of pigment without any fear that it will spread on to the stencil between pulls with the squeegee. Giving oneself a wide border, particularly at each end of the screen, will also make it much easier to complete the stroke, with

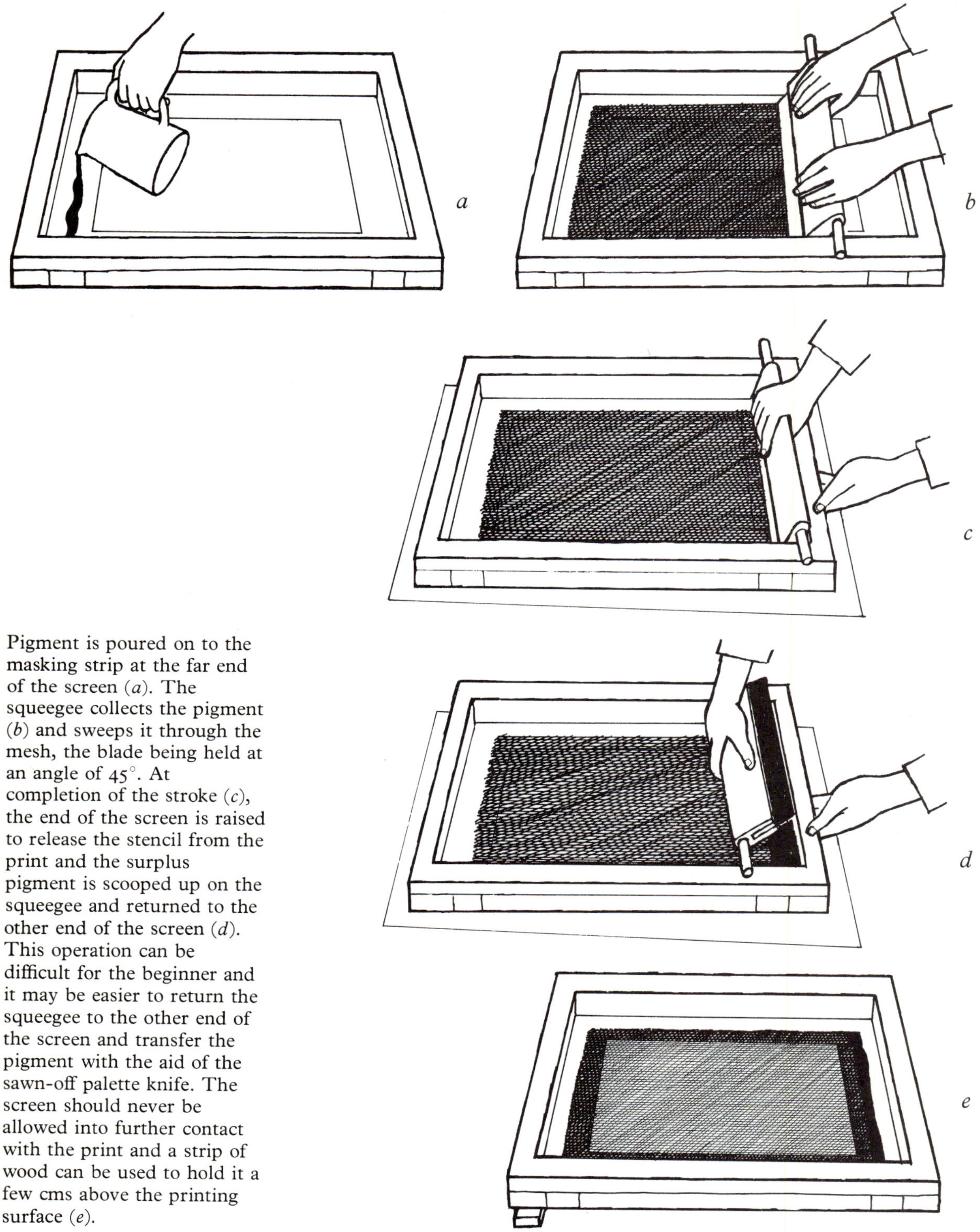

Pigment is poured on to the masking strip at the far end of the screen (*a*). The squeegee collects the pigment (*b*) and sweeps it through the mesh, the blade being held at an angle of 45°. At completion of the stroke (*c*), the end of the screen is raised to release the stencil from the print and the surplus pigment is scooped up on the squeegee and returned to the other end of the screen (*d*). This operation can be difficult for the beginner and it may be easier to return the squeegee to the other end of the screen and transfer the pigment with the aid of the sawn-off palette knife. The screen should never be allowed into further contact with the print and a strip of wood can be used to hold it a few cms above the printing surface (*e*).

the squeegee held at the same angle throughout. The best angle for the blade of the squeegee is about 45° to the plane of the printing surface. If the screen is a small one, it is possible to make the squeegee stroke with only one hand whilst the other hand is used to steady the screen. When using a larger screen it is helpful to have an assistant to hold the screen in order that the printer can have two hands free to control the squeegee. When the stage is reached where the screen is locked to a vacuum table the assistant is no longer necessary. In fabric printing there is no way of locking the screen in place for each print (unless one is lucky enough to have access to a professional fabric printing table with a track down each side, by means of which the spacing of the screen can be controlled). The fabric printer will always need an assistant, not only to help him hold the screen but also to help him locate it in the correct position.

One of the most important factors contributing to the successful use of the squeegee is the consistency of the pigment. It is very difficult to make a good print if the pigment is too liquid or too thick. Generally speaking a pigment which will *just* dribble from a container is about right, although there will be some variation between one type of pigment and another, one kind of printing surface and another.

Most people find it easier to draw the squeegee towards them than to push it away from them, so the main printing stroke will be made with a pulling action. The pigment will, of course, need to be returned to the further end of the screen ready for the next pull. This means that, in effect, each print is completed with two strokes of the squeegee. The use of a random number of strokes for each print is to be discouraged since this not only wastes time but can lead to variations in colour intensity, particularly when printing on fabric. Frankly if more than one stroke is required to produce a satisfactory print then there is something seriously wrong either with the stencil or the consistency of the pigment.

The creation of space between the mesh and the surface to be printed is essential for fine printmaking. This 'snap off' distance prevents the stencil from remaining in contact with the printing surface for more than a split second thus avoiding any possibility of the pigment spreading on to areas where it is not wanted. This distance is produced either by locking the screen into the holding device at a distance above the table, or by resting the screen on two strips of wood

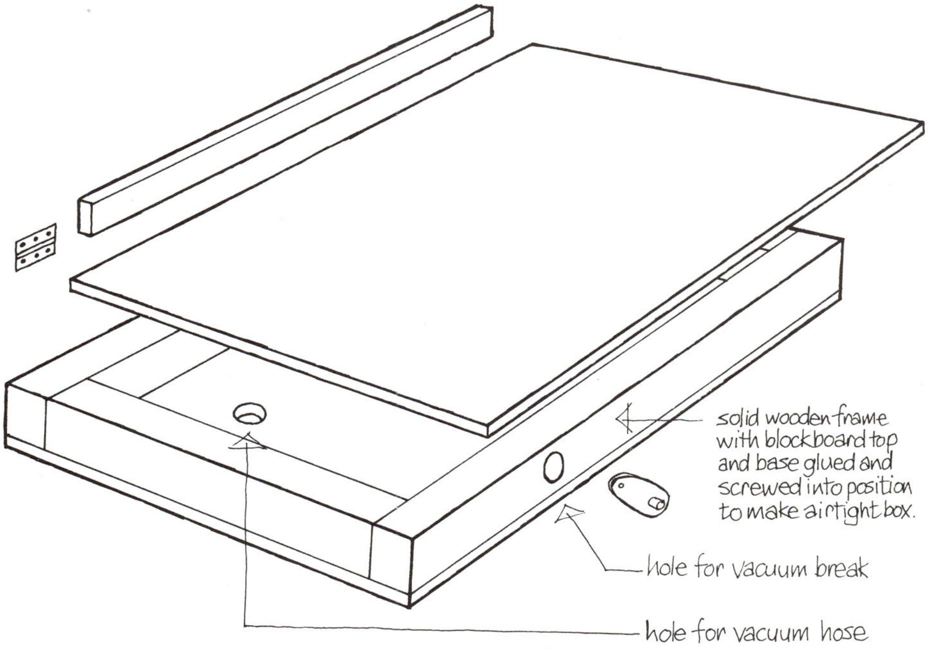

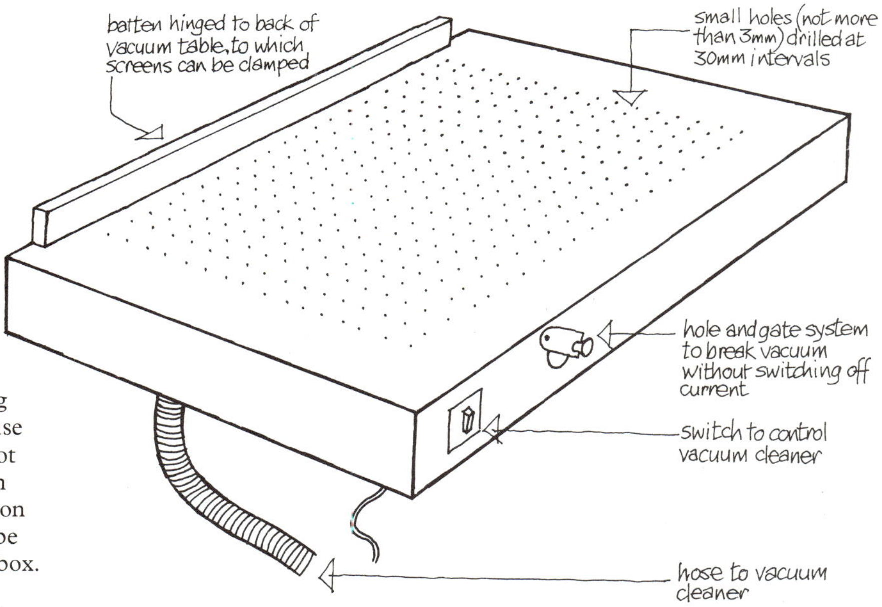

A simple vacuum printing table. It is important to use components which will not warp. A domestic vacuum cleaner provides the suction and a vacuum break can be built into the side of the box. This saves straining the motor by constant switching off and on. A laminated plastic top makes for easy cleaning. Holes larger than 3 mm will cause dimples to form in the paper.

Printing and registration

Registration (accurate control of overprinting) in the production of multi-coloured prints is of great importance, whether one is using the same screen a number of times or a different screen for each colour. For much of the experimental work described so far, over-printing effects can be achieved by locating the screen over the previous print by eye, using the unblocked areas of the screen as a kind of 'window'.

In situations where one is using the same screen in a slightly modified form for the second colour, it can help to draw a line round the screen very lightly in pencil, marking its position on the printing paper. As crude as this may seem it does work quite well provided, of course, that the screen does not need to be turned round.

When really accurate, controlled registration is required it becomes necessary to employ some kind of system both for holding the printing paper firmly in position and for locating the screen each time in an identical position in relation to the paper on the printing table.

The first of these two problems is generally solved by providing an intermittent vacuum which holds the paper firmly to the printing surface. Vacuum tables can be purchased ready made from screen printing suppliers (see page 119), but can be constructed on a do-it-yourself basis requiring only very basic carpentry skill. A design for just such a table appears on page 38. Systems for locating each successive sheet of paper on the printing table are also indicated on page 40. There are a number of methods that can be devised by means of which the screen can be hinged to the table during printing but which enable the screen to be removed and replaced in exactly the position when needed for subsequent prints. The most simple method consists of nothing more than a pair of hinges which are permanently screwed to the baseboard and can be screwed in turn to the screens as they are required for printing. More sophisticated arrangements allow for the more rapid removal and replacement of the screens and incorporate adjustable counterbalances.

A simple way of ensuring that each sheet of printing paper is located in exactly the same position in relation to the screen. For each successive colour it will be necessary to re-staple the card strips to the baseboard to coincide with the position of the new screen

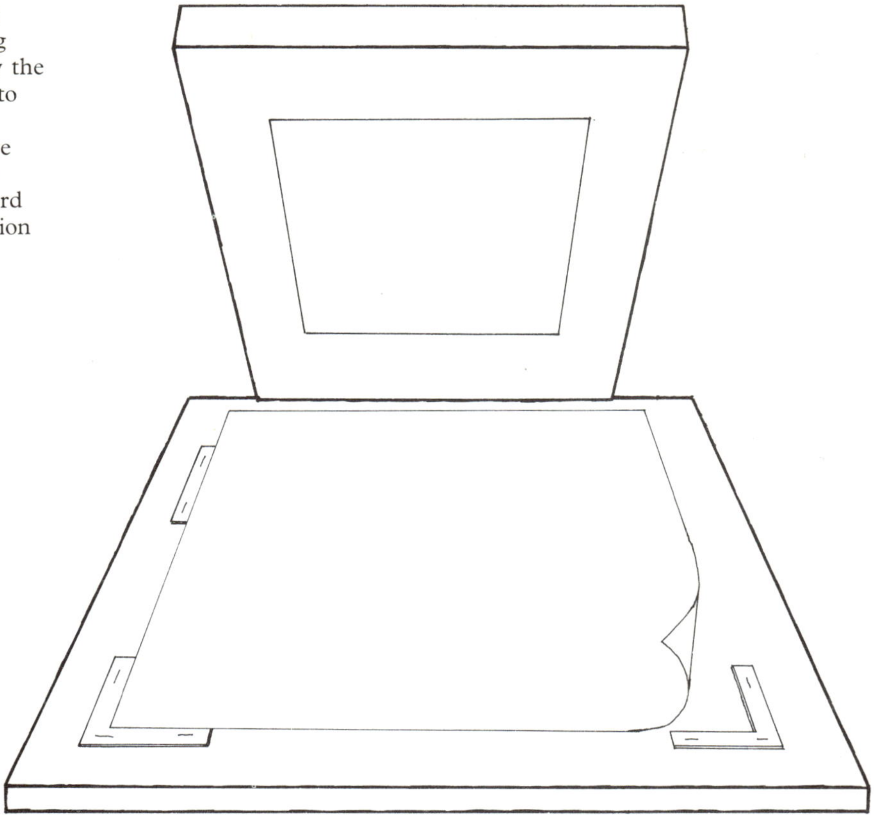

printing paper located accurately into cardboard guides stapled to baseboard.

Holding the screen in a raised position whilst inserting the paper can be achieved in numerous ways. A pivoted 'leg' can be attached to the side of the screen but this tends to obstruct the printing paper. Probably the best system involves the counterbalancing device illustrated on page 42. The system shown here is easy to construct and works very well. A flexible spring can be incorporated into the cord between the screen and the supporting post which makes it possible to depress the screen into the printing position without releasing the toggle

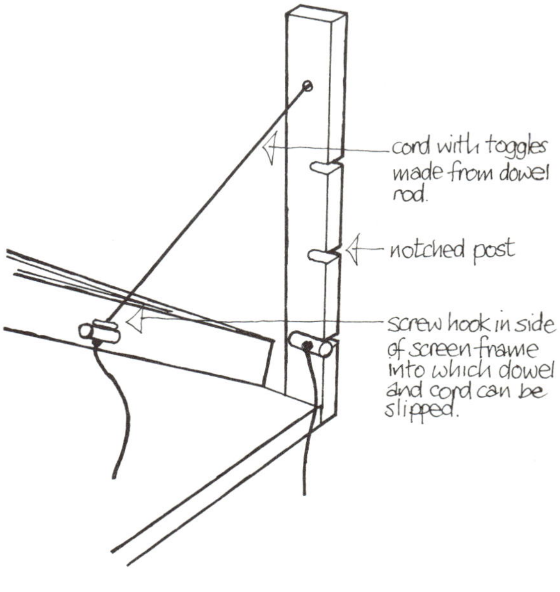

Examples of a number of these different methods are illustrated on page 42.

Whilst it is quite possible to make perfectly good prints on an ordinary flat table, there are many advantages to be gained from the use of a vacuum printing table. The vacuum table holds the paper so firmly in place that it is possible to create what is known as 'snap distance' between the mesh and the paper. In other words the mesh is only in contact with the paper for the brief moment that the squeegee is passing that particular point on the screen (see diagram page 42). In this way, pigment is prevented from spreading under the stencil, a common cause of smudged prints. To create snap distance strips of thin card are placed under the screen frame, the exact thickness of the card depending to some extent on the size of the screen and the tension of the mesh. It is important to remember to allow for snap distance when locking the screen into the hingeing apparatus.

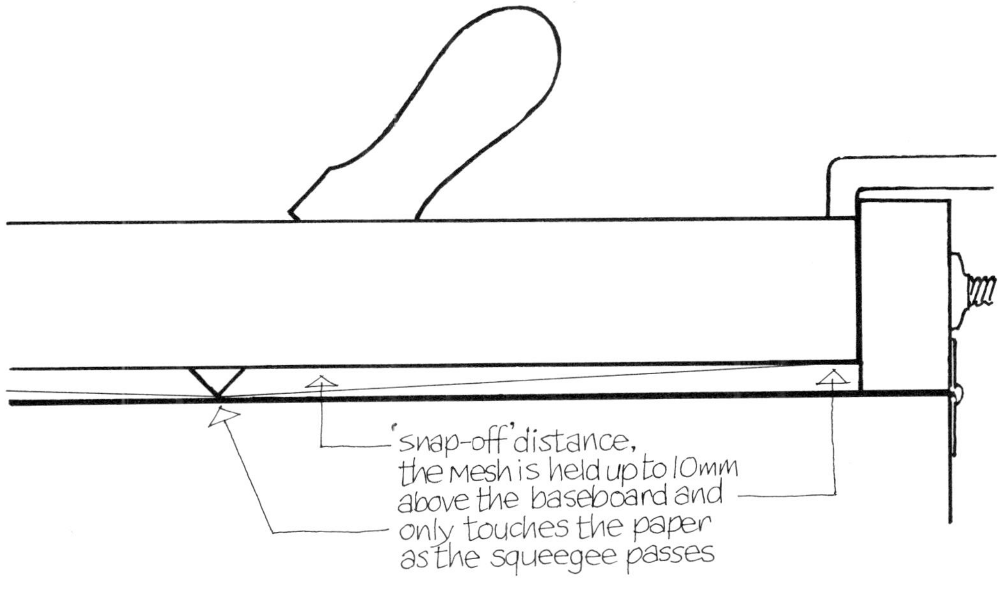

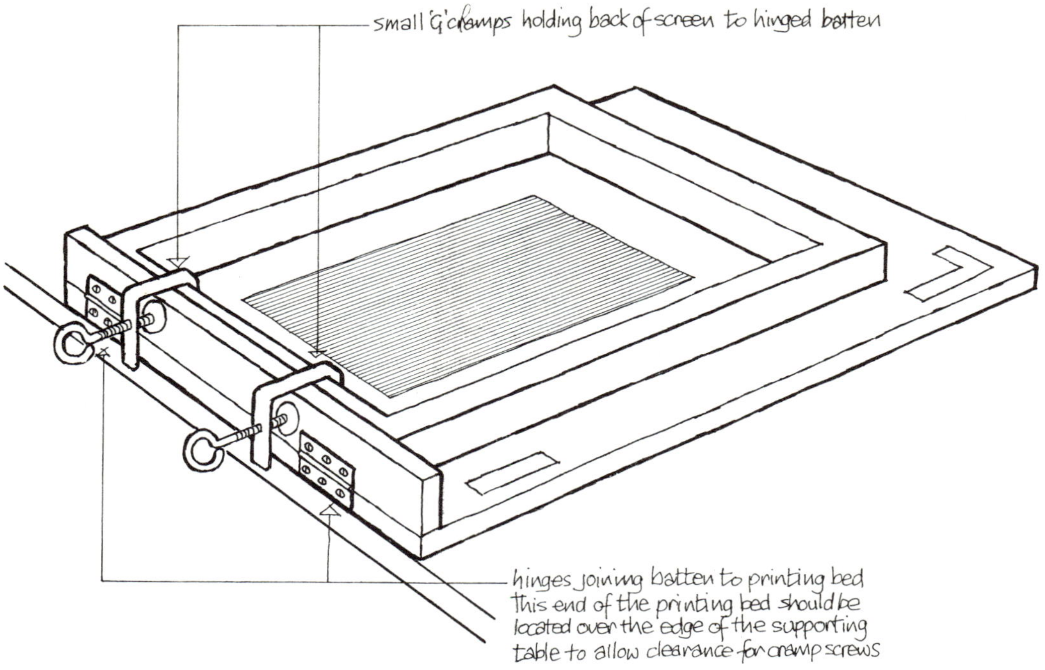
small 'G' cramps holding back of screen to hinged batten
hinges joining batten to printing bed
This end of the printing bed should be located over the edge of the supporting table to allow clearance for cramp screws

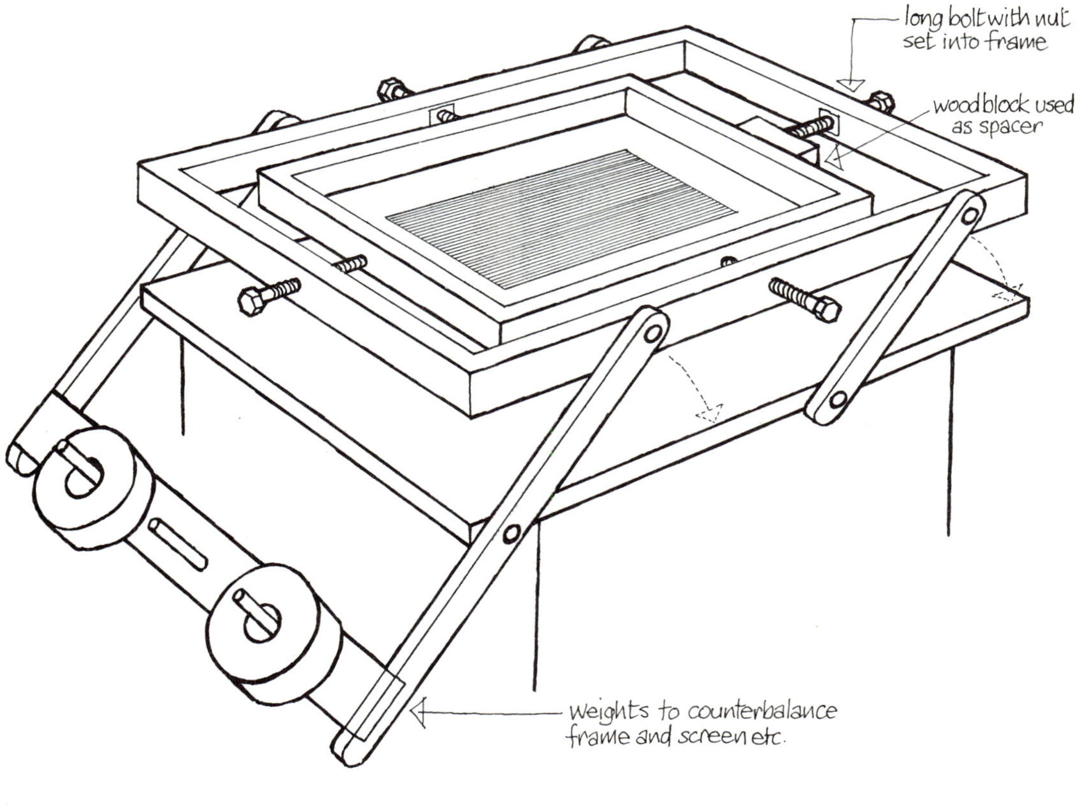
long bolt with nut set into frame
woodblock used as spacer
weights to counterbalance frame and screen etc.

Textures

In the context of printmaking a texture can be defined as a variation of surface, and as such is often required as a component part of a design or as a background to which more work will be added at a later stage. Screen printing is a useful medium for producing textured papers or other materials for use subsequently in making collage pictures. I have also used screens to provide textural effects in acrylic painting. Almost certainly the reader's early experiments will produce a number of failures, these should not be thrown away but can be stored for future use in other design activities, such as collages, fabric designs, etc.

With the exercise of a little inventiveness and imagination it is possible to devise an almost endless number of ways of texturing a screen or parts of a screen. Here are just a few:

1 Liquid paraffin wax can be splashed or splattered onto the mesh as indeed can any other suitable stopping-out liquid.

2 Rubbings can be made in solid wax directly onto the mesh from interesting, uneven surfaces such as planks of timber (planks rescued from the sea are particularly good for this purpose), textured plastic and glass, or old worn pavings.

3 Potato or other block prints can be made directly onto the mesh using gum or PVA.

4 Gum or PVA applied with decorator's rollers.

5 Rubber cement can be spread unevenly over the mesh, coated with gelatine, gum or some other form of water-based glue. When the glue is dry the cement can be removed with cement thinner or petroleum – making sure that all normal fire precautions are observed.

6 Wax rubbings can also be coated with glue and the wax removed.

7 Gum or some other stopping out liquid can be sprayed onto the mesh through a grid, eg a perforated zinc sheet, fine wire mesh, etc.

Examples of some of these techniques are included in the illustrations.

Opposite above There are many ways that can be devised to hinge the screen to the printing table, ranging from the use of door hinges which are screwed directly into the screen frame before each printing run to the very sophisticated arrangements built into the professional vacuum table. For cheapness and simplicity the method illustrated here is one of the best

Opposite below An ingenious screen printing table made and used by the boys in an Essex boarding school. This system has the advantage of lifting the whole screen clear of the baseboard thus facilitating the location of the printing paper

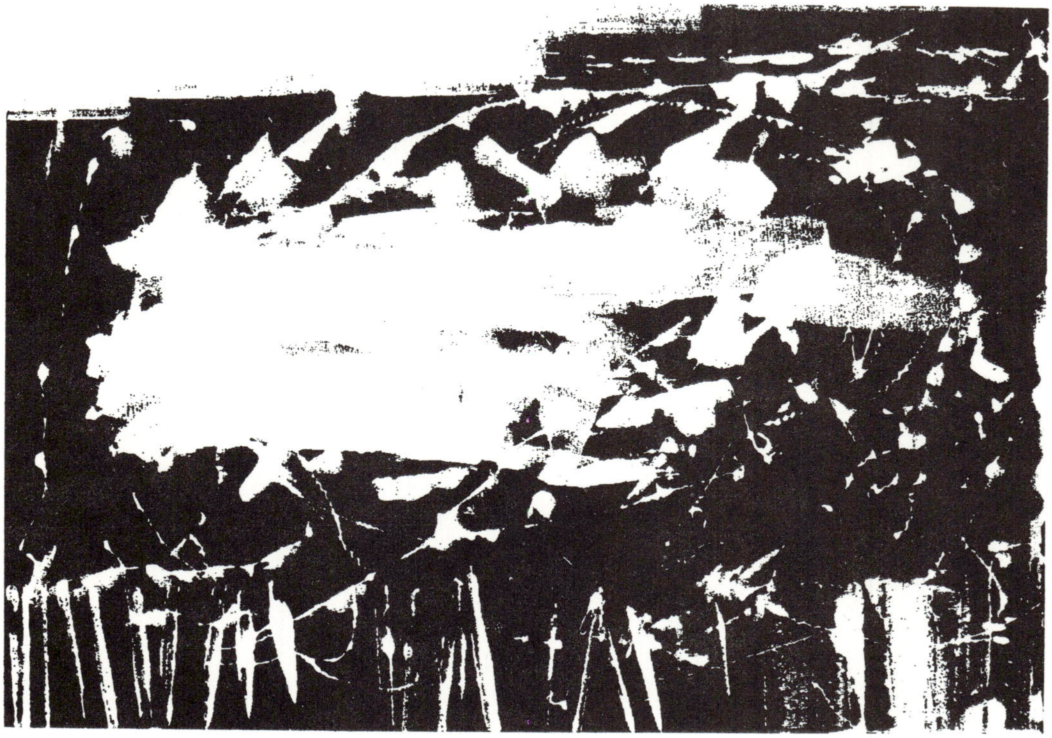

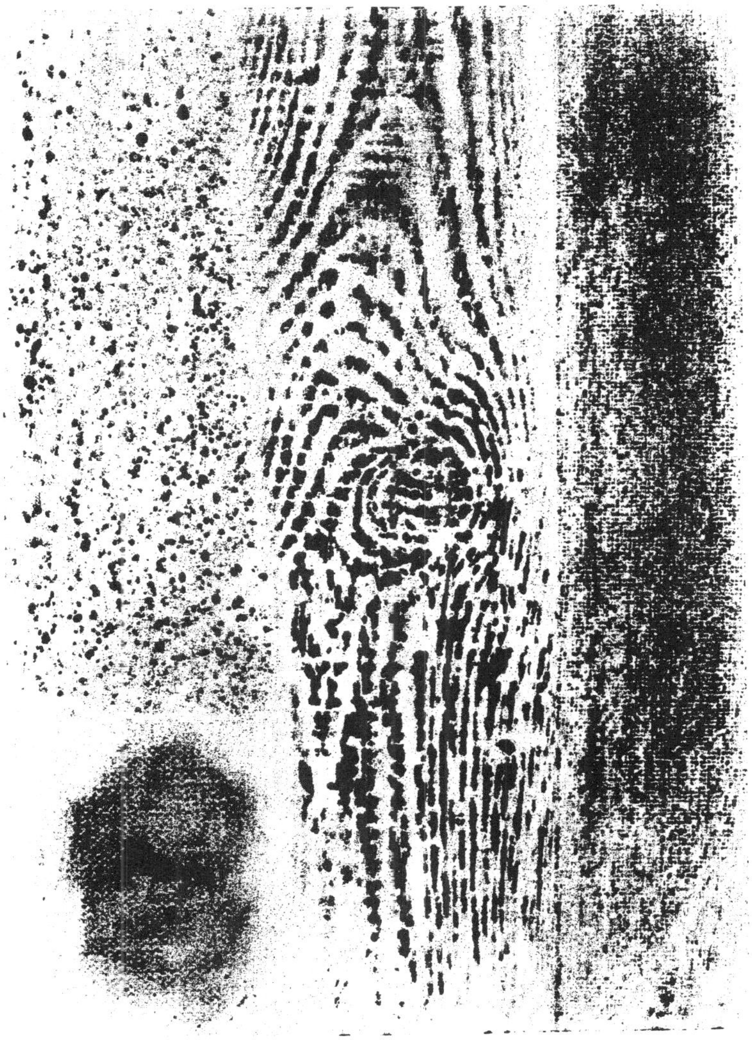

A piece of solid paraffin wax used to make rubbings of various textured surfaces directly onto the screen. It was then coated with gelatine and potassium dichromate, allowed to dry hard and the wax then removed with a warm iron

Opposite above Texture produced by applying gum to a screen with a sponge

Opposite below Texture produced by dribbling 'green' screen filler onto the screen and spreading it with a piece of card

The stages in making a screen from an ordinary photograph. Part of the original photograph

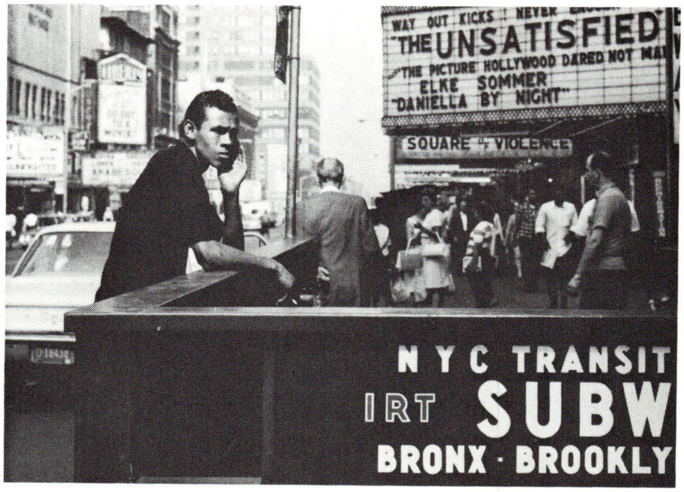

Transformation into a *Kodalith* print by projecting the negative onto translucent printing paper. This requires a darkroom etc (see Suppliers) but is similar to normal processing. A positive print is produced in which all intermediate tones have been resolved to black or white

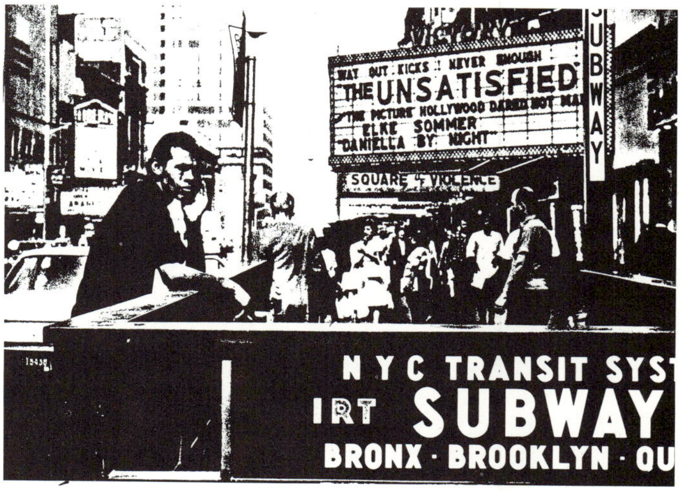

The *Kodalith* print is contacted with a gelatine and potassium dichromate prepared screen and treated as described on page 47. The success of the process depends greatly on the quality of the original photograph but the results are often quite exciting

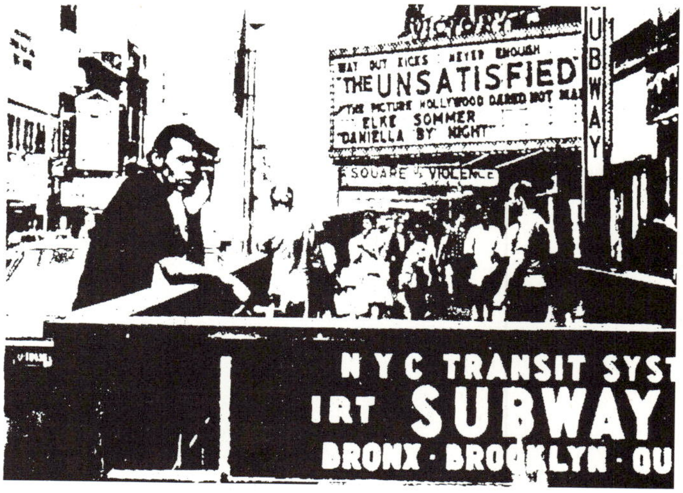

Producing a screen photographically

Screen printing can be used as a creative/expressive process very much as one would use any other direct graphic process, exploiting the characteristics of the craft and developing the imagery in response to the particular properties of the medium; or it can be used simply as a means of reproducing an existing image. So far in this book I have concentrated on the first of these two aspects.

However the development of photo-screen processes has provided the studio printmaker with the ability to reproduce almost any image he desires, however complex or detailed, using only the most basic equipment. Indeed this has brought about a situation in which it is now difficult to define just exactly what is an artist's print, and many works are sold in limited editions which could more accurately be described as 'reproductions'; the artist taking little further part in their production once he has provided the original design for the professional printers to work upon.

Photo-screen making exploits the fact that certain substances when sensitised with particular chemicals and exposed to light – particularly ultra-violet light – become insoluble in water. This means that a screen can be coated with such a substance and exposed to light behind a transparent, positive image. The light hardens the coating on which the image permits it to fall and when the whole surface is subjected to a spray of warm water the unhardened areas – corresponding to the black images in the original positive – are washed away, thus providing a screen which when printed will reproduce the original design.

It all sounds very simple and in essence it is. However because the process is in such demand by the printing industry, the suppliers of photo-sensitive materials are constantly refining their materials and processes so that to the beginner there seems to be a confusing range of possibilities open to them. Much of this photo-sensitive stencil material is designed for very specialised use, to reproduce very small lettering, to withstand very long printing runs, to print on very specialised surfaces or with very specialised pigments. The studio printmaker can, in practice, ignore many of the more sophisticated photo-sensitive products and confine himself to one or two basic techniques.

Essentially there are two ways of coating a screen with a light sensitive medium. One can use a liquid which is spread onto the mesh and allowed to dry before being exposed to light; or one can use any one of a wide range of sheet or indirect stencils most of which are pressed into place on the mesh after they have been exposed to light and washed out. In this book I intend to concentrate attention on the first of these two processes because it is much cheaper and generally provides a screen which will satisfy all the requirements of the beginner. Should the reader wish to experiment with indirect stencils it would be to his advantage to consult one or other of the manufacturers listed at the end of the book, all of whom provide very comprehensive instructions on the use of their products.

Photo-sensitive emulsions

Until the development of synthetic emulsions such as PVA, natural substances such as gelatine were used as photo-sensitive coatings for screens, and indeed gelatine is still sometimes used. However it exhibits a number of disadvantages compared with PVA. It can only be used in a warmed state – although it must never be boiled – and being a natural, organic substance it is subject to bacterial decay and once mixed, it has a very short shelf life.

On the other hand water-soluble PVA is cheap, stable, requires no preparation and can easily be removed from the screen at the conclusion of the printing run.

Screen printing sundriesmen supply PVAs designed specifically for screen printing but in practice I find it is quite possible to use standard PVA glues, provided that they are of a kind which is soluble again in water once it has been allowed to dry. A number of glues of this kind have been developed to satisfy demands from primary schools for a water-washable glue and are sometimes referred to as 'school glues'. Non-washable PVA glues and mediums are not suitable for photographic screen printing purposes since, although they accept the image, it is virtually impossible to wash out the unexposed areas of glue. School glues are at least half the price of the recognised photo-emulsions and also possess the advantage that, if bought in bulk, they can double as an ordinary studio glue.

A recipe for a photographic emulsion appears on page 116 and the procedure for producing an image on a screen photographically is as follows:

1 A transparent positive of the image to be reproduced must be prepared. This can consist of a photographic image on an acetate sheet (one is tempted to say a photographic negative but this would be misleading as, for reasons which will be explained later, the image must in terms of blacks and whites be identical to the one to be reproduced) or it can consist of something as simple as a drawing in black paint on a sheet of tracing paper.

2 PVA emulsion is mixed with potassium dichromate in the proportions indicated in the recipe on page 116.

3 A screen which has been stretched and thoroughly scoured and allowed to dry is coated with the PVA (see illustration page 92).

4 Once coated, the screen is dried in relative darkness. A photographic darkroom is ideal for this process should one be available; however the emulsion is only really sensitive to ultra-violet light so the drying can be done anywhere away from daylight or fluorescent light – in the light of a 20 watt tungsten bulb for example. The screen will dry naturally overnight but drying can be accelerated by the use of a hair dryer or fan-assisted electric fire. The emulsion should be dried by the warm air and must not itself become heated. It is advisable to expose the screen as soon as possible after drying, certainly within a few hours.

5 The 'sandwich' of screen, image, glass and support is assembled in the subdued light and transferred to the light box for exposure (see illustrations pages 54, 55).

6 Once exposed, the screen is washed out in warm water which removes the unexposed emulsion. The screen is then allowed to dry.

7 The dry screen is checked for 'pin-holes' or other faults and if necessary touched up and or masked with brown paper tape.

8 The screen is now ready for printing and will be suitable for most types of pigment.

9 To remove the emulsion coating at the end of the printing run, use screen stripper or immerse in domestic bleach. This can be accomplished by putting the screen mesh down on a formica-topped table and allowing it to rest for about ten minutes in a puddle of bleach before washing out in water. All traces of the printing pigment must be removed before attempting to remove emulsion.

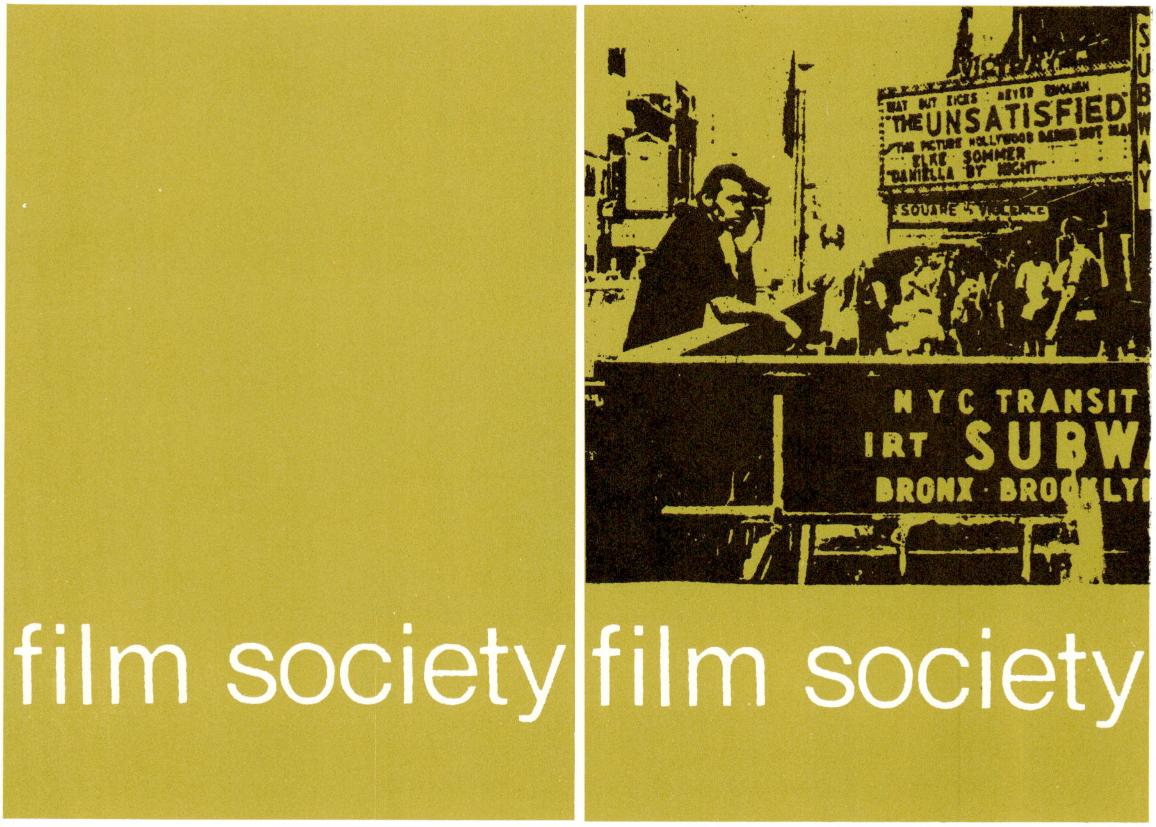

Film society poster, using the photographically-produced screen described on page 46. The background was printed from an open screen, on the inside of which the words were applied with instant lettering. If possible, such lettering should be sprayed with a special aerosol fixative, care being taken not to spray too closely and block the screen

Take care when positioning the positive transparency on the mesh, to ensure that the design will be transferred to the screen the correct way round. This may seem rather obvious, but in the excitement of carrying out the various stages in the photographic process, which sometimes involve inverting the screen, it is all too easy to make this mistake and end up with lettering which can only be read in a mirror.

Photographic screen techniques are capable of almost infinite refinement. It is even possible to make quite an acceptable screen directly from a photographic colour slide (diapositive) by projecting the slide onto the sensitised screen as if it were a projection screen. The amount of the slide that actually reproduces will depend a great deal on the subject, and it must be remembered that screen emulsions are orthochromatic and will not respond to the red end of the spectrum. However given a reasonable exposure time and a slide projector fitted with a

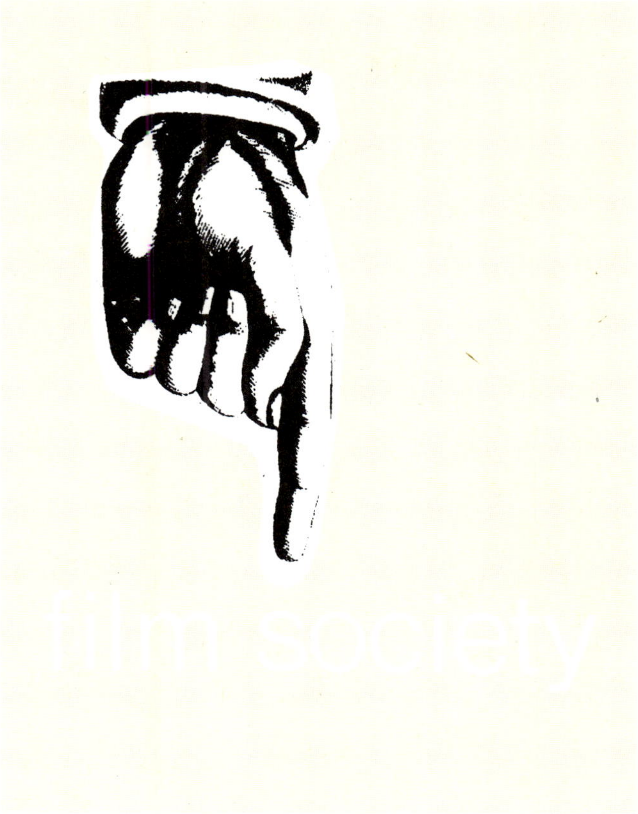

quartz iodide or 'QI' bulbs, as most modern projectors are, then some very interesting results are possible.

Using professionally produced positive transparencies on fine, high quality meshes, the most detailed and intricate work is possible, but a great deal of satisfaction can be derived from making screens photographically from a whole assortment of prints, rubbings and other translucent materials, achieving effects impossible by any other printing method.

Another variation of the film society notice, using a photographically-made screen from an antique printer's 'fist'

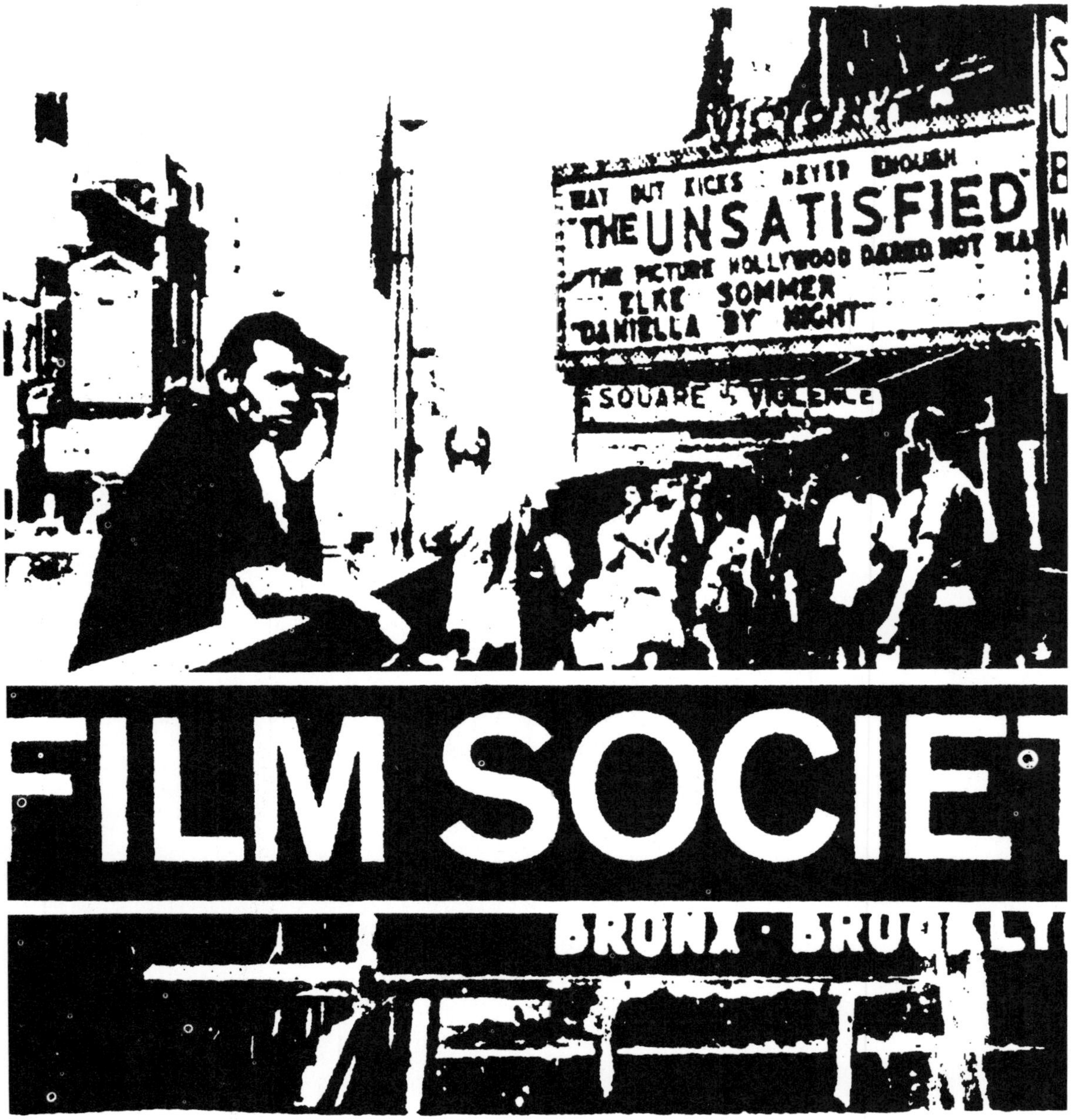

Another use for the photographically produced screen. In this instance the screen was printed with a paper strip across the middle which produced a white area which was later filled by another screen containing the wording, again using instant lettering

The light box

For the perfect exposure of either direct or indirect photosensitive stencils, a controlled source of light is required which is cool, bright and high in ultra violet content. It is possible to expose PVA and potassium dichromate in sunlight but this source is uncontrollable and, particularly in the UK, quite unpredictable. In order to be certain of the correct degree of hardening one needs to be in control of both the intensity of the light and its distance from the stencil material to be exposed. Since it is necessary to expose the emulsion as soon as possible after it has dried one cannot simply hang about waiting for the sun to come out.

The answer lies in the construction of a light box along the lines of one of those illustrated on pages 54, 55. Tungsten light is not very suitable for the exposure of screen stencils; it is low in ultra violet and tungsten lamps of sufficient intensity would generate far too much heat. This heat would have an adverse effect on the emulsion.

A light box can be designed either to illuminate the stencil from above or from below. Although one can use a battery of 'daylight' strip lights, and this is the safest form of illumination, an HPR 125 watt mercury vapour lamp, plus control gear, is by far the most convenient and effective light source. A mercury vapour lamp needs to be treated with respect from the safety point of view, but as a kit the lamp is not expensive and is easily assembled into a unit. Exposure time will vary with the nature of the stencil being exposed; a rough guide would be approximately two minutes at a distance of 50 cm.

The UV lamp has its own built-in reflector but, obviously, there is a limit to the area that can be illuminated to an equal intensity by one bulb. It may, therefore, be necessary to mount more than one bulb unit in an assembly if very large stencils are to be exposed.

The intense light from a mercury vapour lamp can cause eye damage and the ultra violent content of the light can injure the

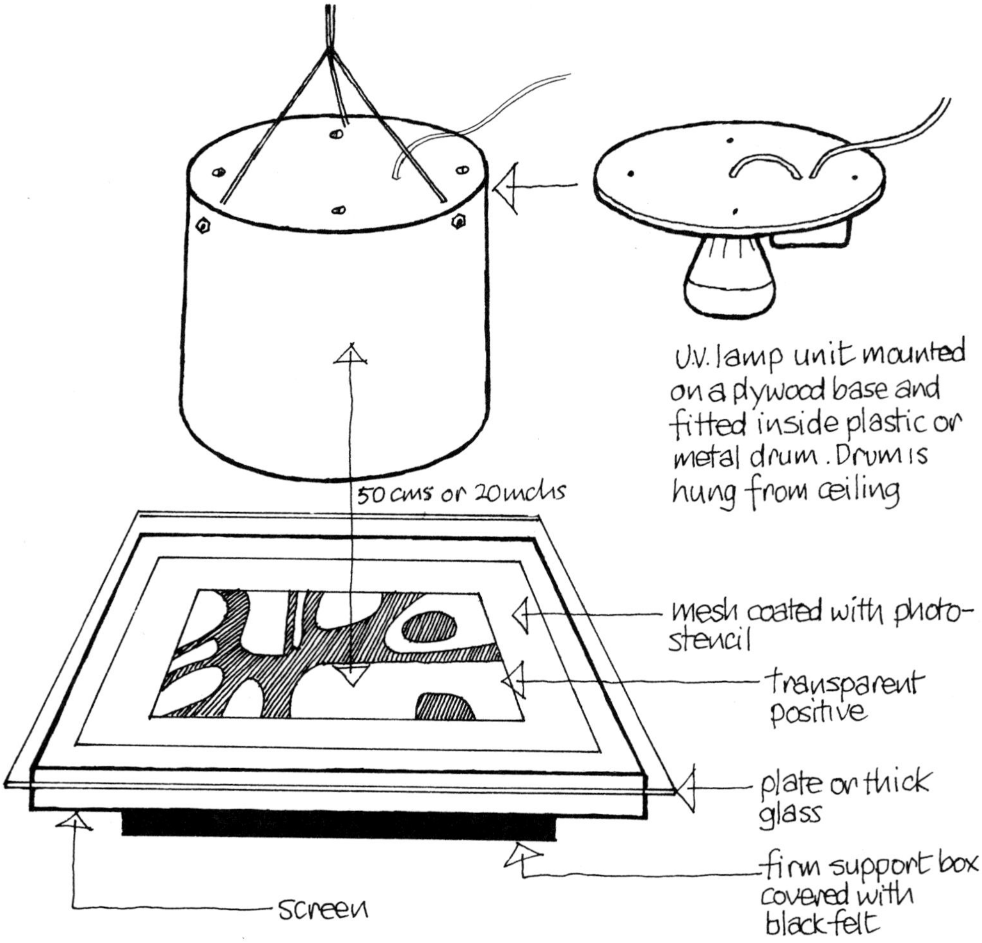

An overhead exposure lamp with the UV lamp unit fitted into a plastic or metal tub. Plastic is ideal from the electrical safety point of view, and since UV lamps give out virtually no heat there is no danger of the plastic being burned or distorted

skin if exposure is protracted. When working with a UV lamp it is advisable to wear dark glasses and the stencil should never be held in place by hand. In an educational establishment it is important to guard against accidental injury to visiting students and others who may happen to wander casually into the room when exposure is taking place.

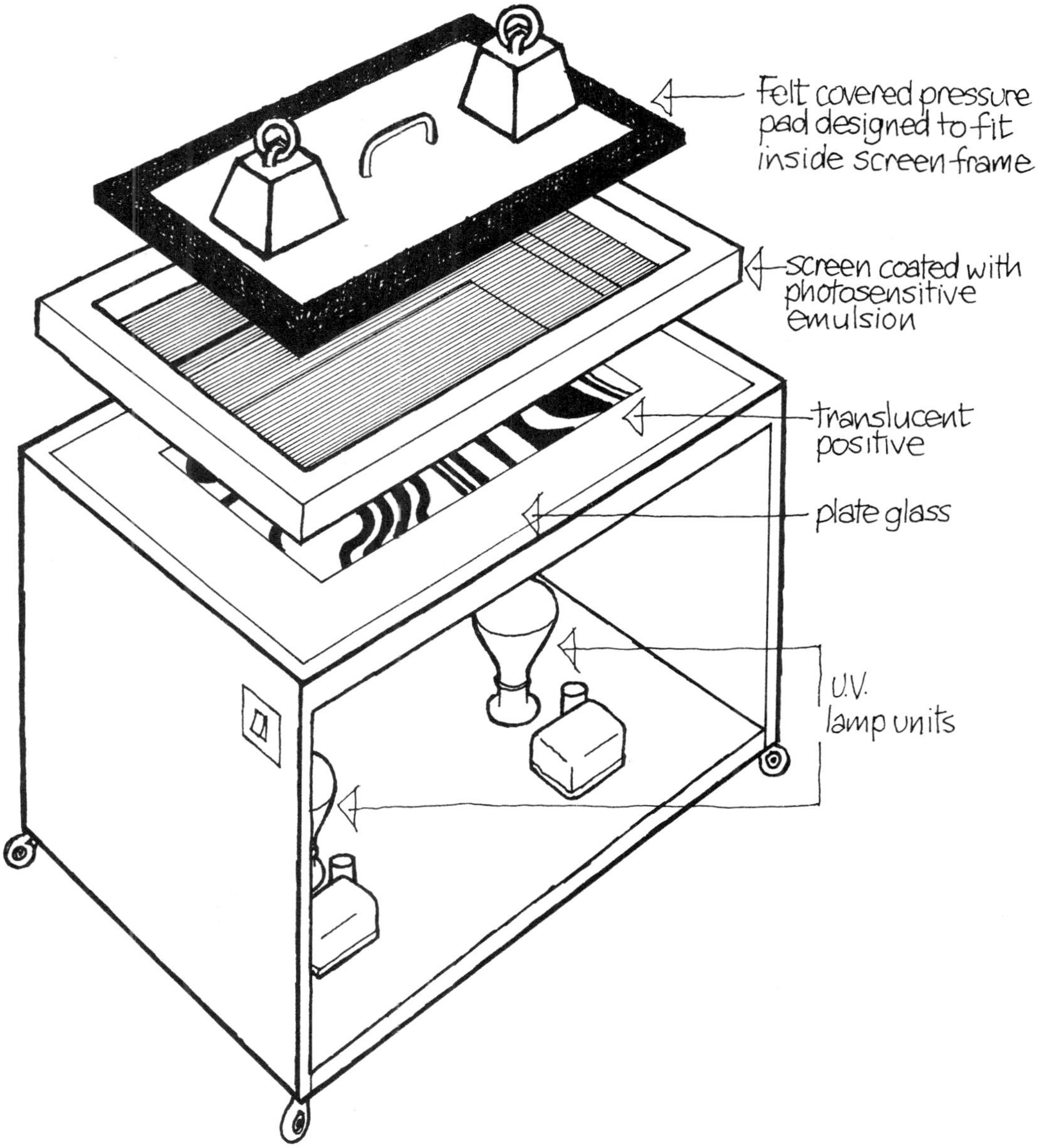

A light-box can be constructed directly from heavy plywood or chipboard, or a framed construction can be clad in thinner material. Two lamp units can be included to ensure even exposure of large stencils

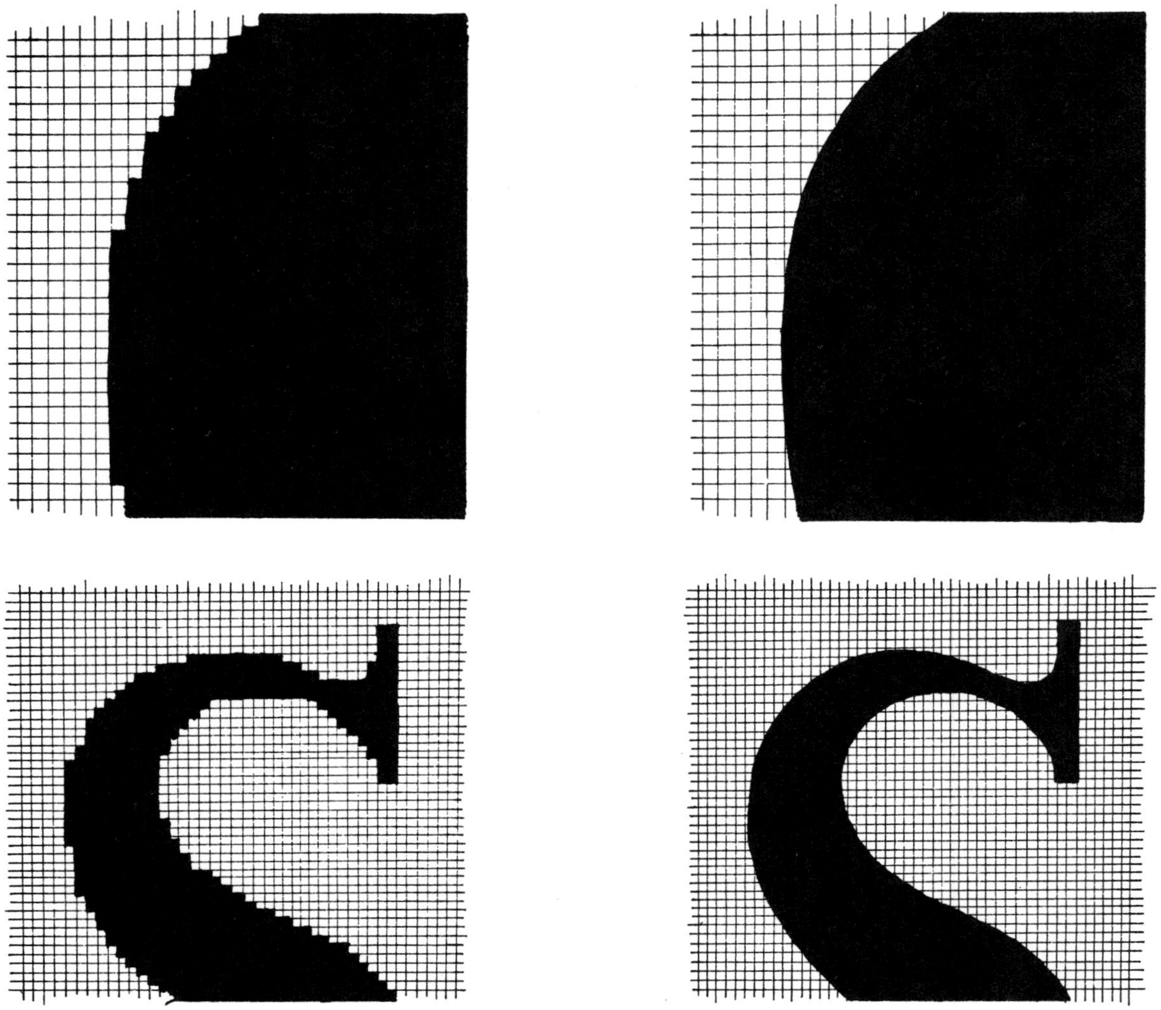

A liquid direct stencil will tend to cling to the squares of the mesh causing the sawtoothing effect illustrated by these diagrams. In practice this only becomes a problem when reproducing very fine detail such as small lettering, and can be mitigated by using a finer mesh

Posters and other graphics

Although screen printing is now one of the most widely used processes in the whole field of commercial and industrial printing and design, the equipment used by the professional differs very little from that described in this book, as basic as that may seem. And in terms of the screen process itself, as distinct from supportive resources such as the production of high quality half-tone positives, etc, there is virtually nothing that the professional can do, that cannot be done equally well by the private artist working in his own studio.

The professional printer is, of course, interested in speed and mass-production and any modification of his equipment as compared with that employed by the studio printmaker is directed to that end.

Many readers will be interested in the production of posters and other informative literature, and almost any of the techniques described so far are capable of being used to put lettering on a screen, and the choice of technique will depend on the scale of the lettering to be used and the number of prints required. For example it would not be practical to attempt small lettering using molten wax, nor would wax be suitable as a medium for a long printing run, particularly if one was using a spirit-based pigment. On the other hand for a bold effect which was needed very quickly – say in an educational situation – wax would be ideal. Wax screens could also be used to provide backgrounds onto which lettering could be imposed.

Undoubtedly the most reliable and controllable method of producing a screen poster is the use of photographic techniques allied to instant lettering. The designer can work on transparent film, or even tracing paper and combine instant lettering (see list of suppliers) with images drawn in black paint (indian or drawing ink is not, in my experience, opaque enough). The screen is then made photographically from this positive by the method described earlier. For multi-coloured posters the screen carrying the information can be overprinted on to a previously prepared background or combined with other photographically

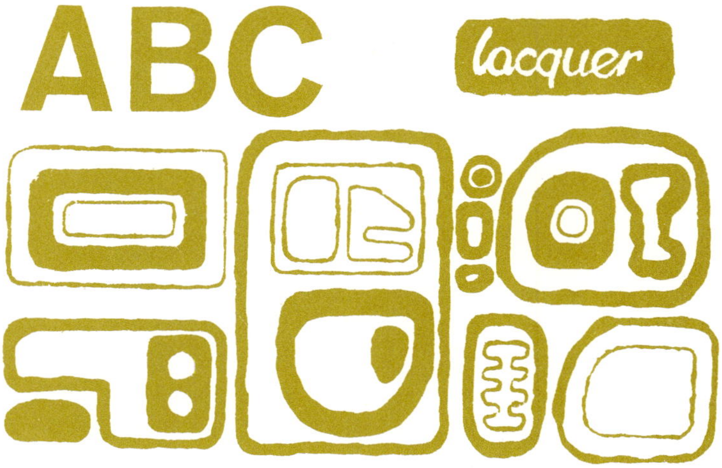

A screen coated on the inside with gelatine was protected from potassium dichromate by screen lacquer and instant lettering. Screen lacquer was used to paint the word 'lacquer' after the screen had been washed out and dried

produced screens using the first positive as a 'master'.

It is possible to make a screen directly by applying plastic lettering to the actual mesh and fixing it in place with the aerosol lacquer supplied by the manufacturer. The fixative must be used sparingly as, being lacquer, it could block the screen. A screen made in this way will produce a negative image, ie white on a coloured background and it must be remembered that all work must be done on the inside of the screen if the printed lettering is to read the right way round. Also, of course, it would not be practical to try to produce very small lettering by this method.

Whilst on the subject of letter size, mention should be made of the limitations of screen printing in this respect. In principle, the limits on the smallness of the type it is possible to reproduce by means of a screen depend on two factors: the fineness of the mesh and the character of the photographic stencil being used. One would assume that in printing a fine poster, good quality ink would be used and therefore the pigment is not really a factor.

For any lettering below about 24 points (9 mm or $\frac{1}{3}$ in.) to be

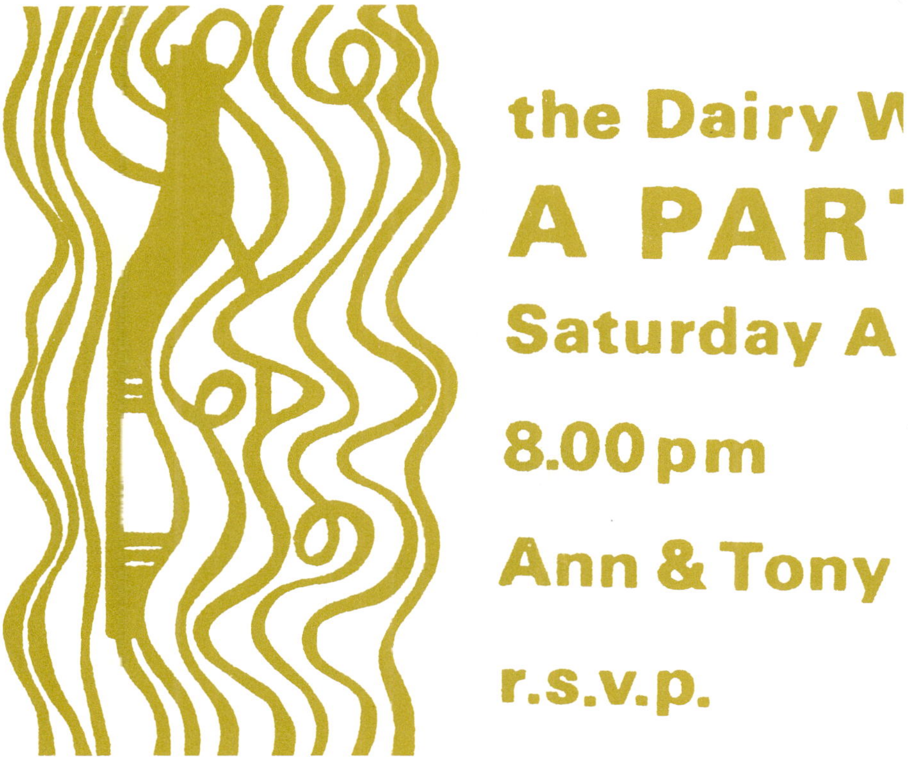

Detail from a party invitation card. The design was made on *Kodatrace* in *Letraset* and black ink and transferred to the screen using direct stencil technique

legible, one should use one of the finer meshes (see page 56). It is also best to use a sheet stencil as this will obviate the 'saw-toothing' which tends to impair the legibility of small lettering. It would also be unwise for the reader to try to reproduce small fancy typefaces such as *Palace script*, or faces with very delicate serifs or heavily contrasted thicks and thins.

However, having said this, it must be admitted that it is remarkable just what one can achieve in the matter of legibility, even using the most unlikely materials.

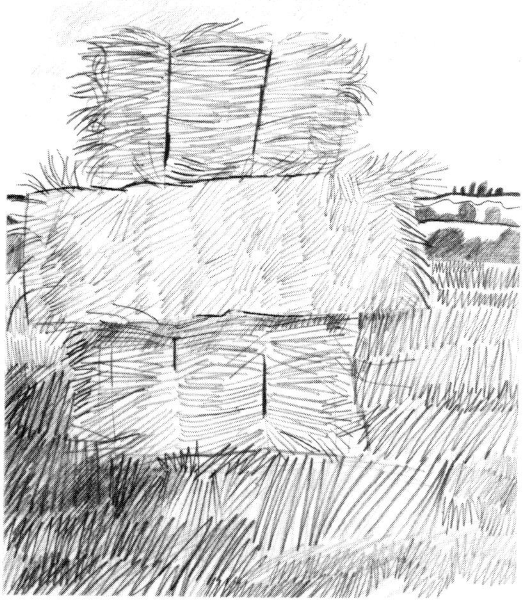

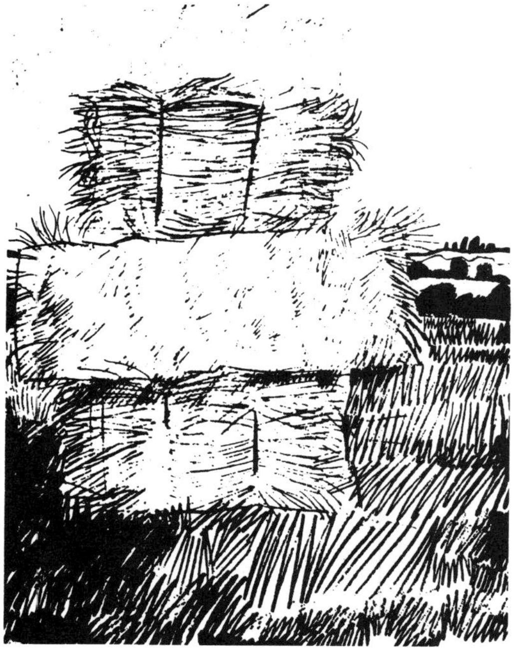

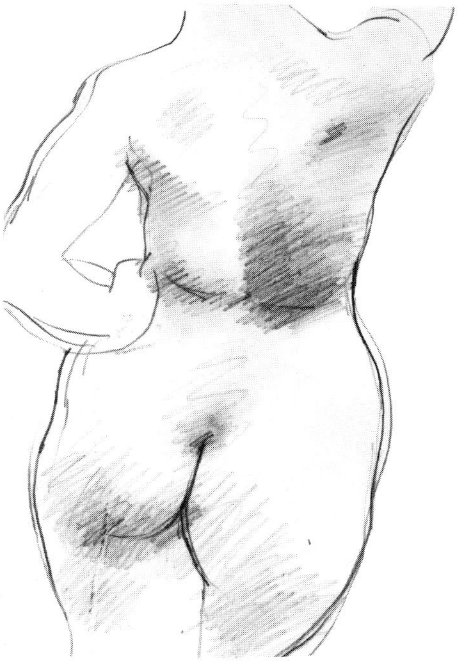

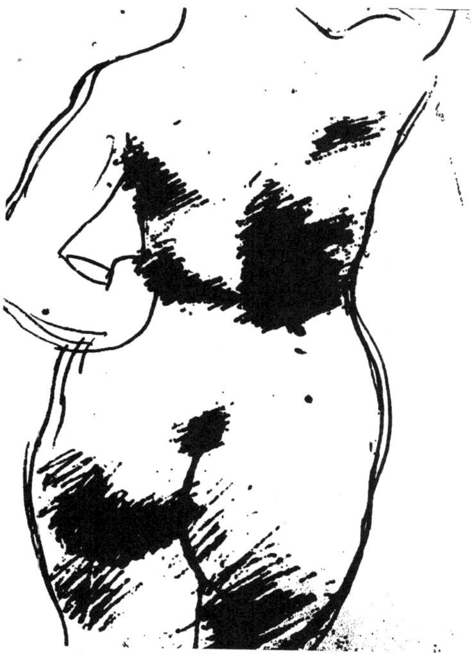

Reproducing illustrations and other artwork

It has already been suggested that given the capacity to produce a screen photographically, the scope of the imagery which it is possible to reproduce depends only on one's ability to provide a suitable translucent positive. As with any other reprographic process, continuous-tone originals, ie originals in which there is a gradual shading from black to white, need to be resolved either into a high-contrast positive or into a dot system. This is the case, whether the final print is to be in monochrome or full colour.

Readers with access to suitable photographic facilities will be able to make their own positives, but positives can be ordered from professional agencies at a price, should this prove necessary. By the time the reader reaches this stage in the development of his craft he will already be quite experienced in the use of more primitive materials and it is advisable to experiment with a wide range of much less sophisticated imagery before investing in costly photo-processing. For example it is possible to oil out a printed image so that it becomes sufficiently translucent to produce a reaction on a sensitised screen. Provided the image is on one side of the paper only, a little light lubricating oil can be rubbed into the paper from the back, rendering the unprinted areas remarkably translucent. With sufficient exposure time it is often possible to produce a very effective screen from such an original. When exposing an oiled paper positive, it is advisable to protect the sensitised mesh from the oiled paper with a sheet of transparent kitchen film.

Finally, my advice to anyone wishing to experiment, in order to discover the relative merits of all the less conventional methods of preparing a positive for photographic transfer to a screen, is that they prepare a number of small examples of

Opposite A figure drawing in pencil was 'oiled out' and made into a direct photo-stencil. Much of the subtlety of the original drawing is lost but in many ways the vitality of the line is increased. More work can be added to the screen before it is printed in its final form. The landscape was treated in a similar way only in this instance a crude 'office duplicator' intermediate negative was made

Overleaf Collage print from images photocopied from a magazine on an office photocopier

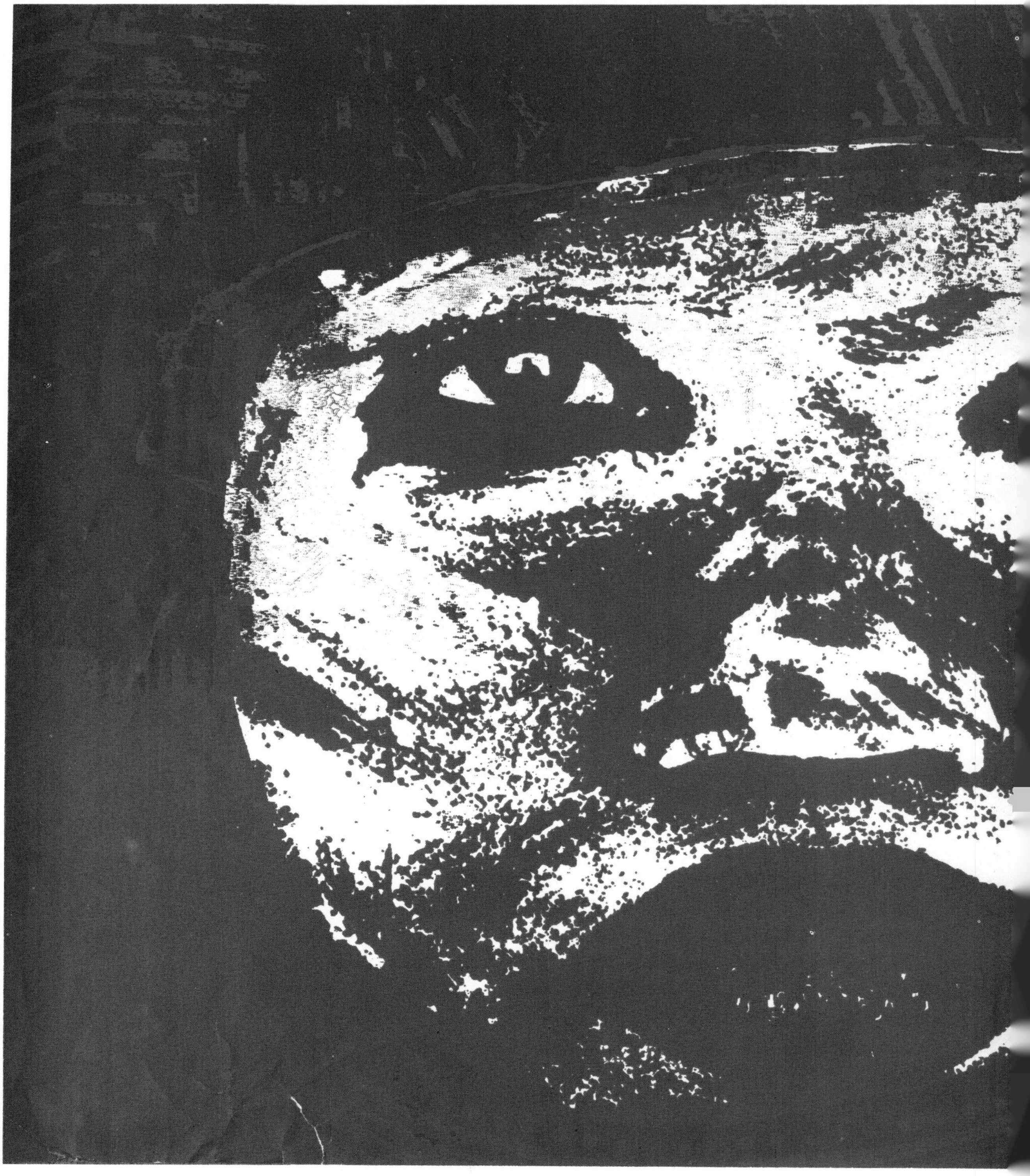

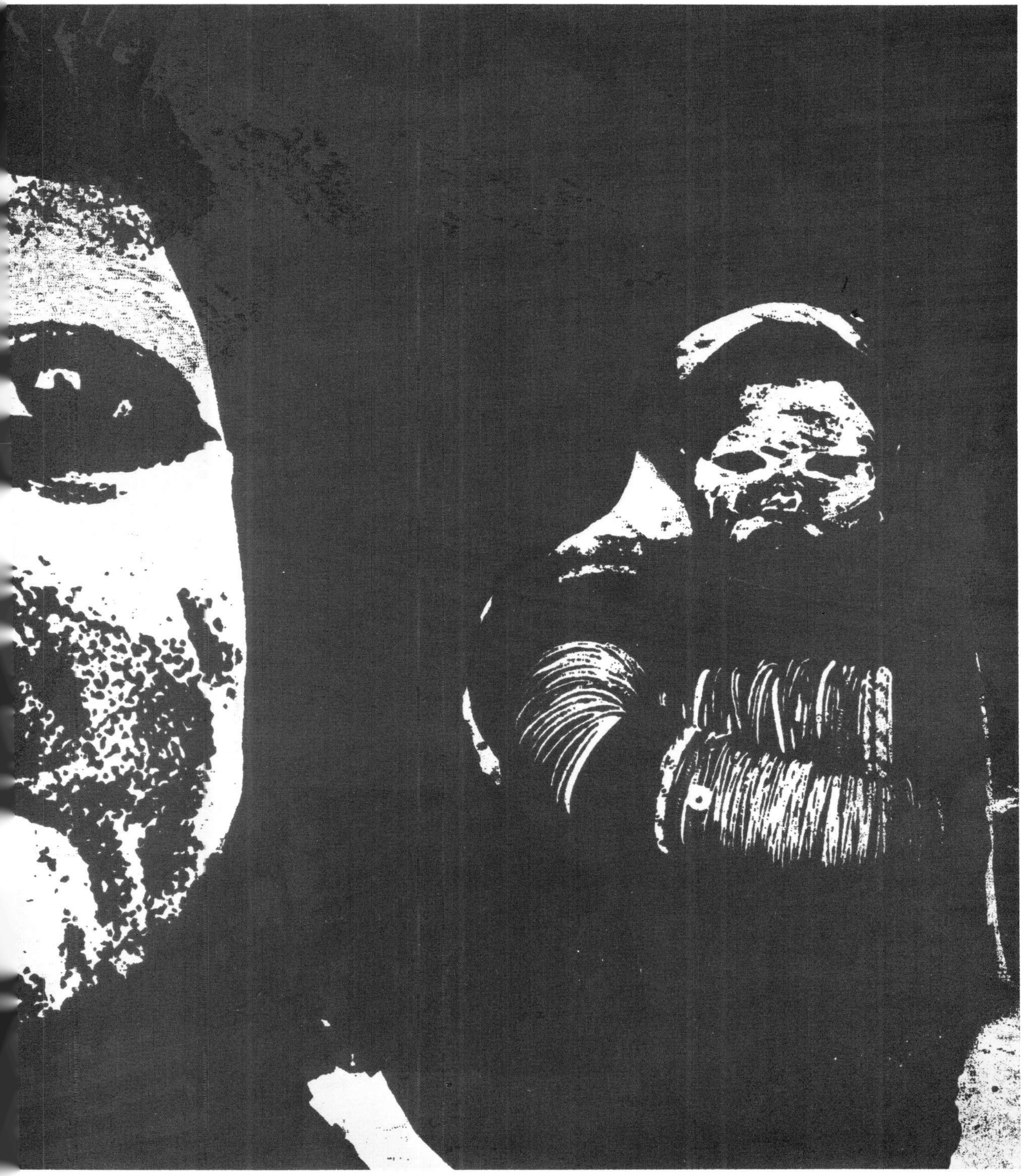

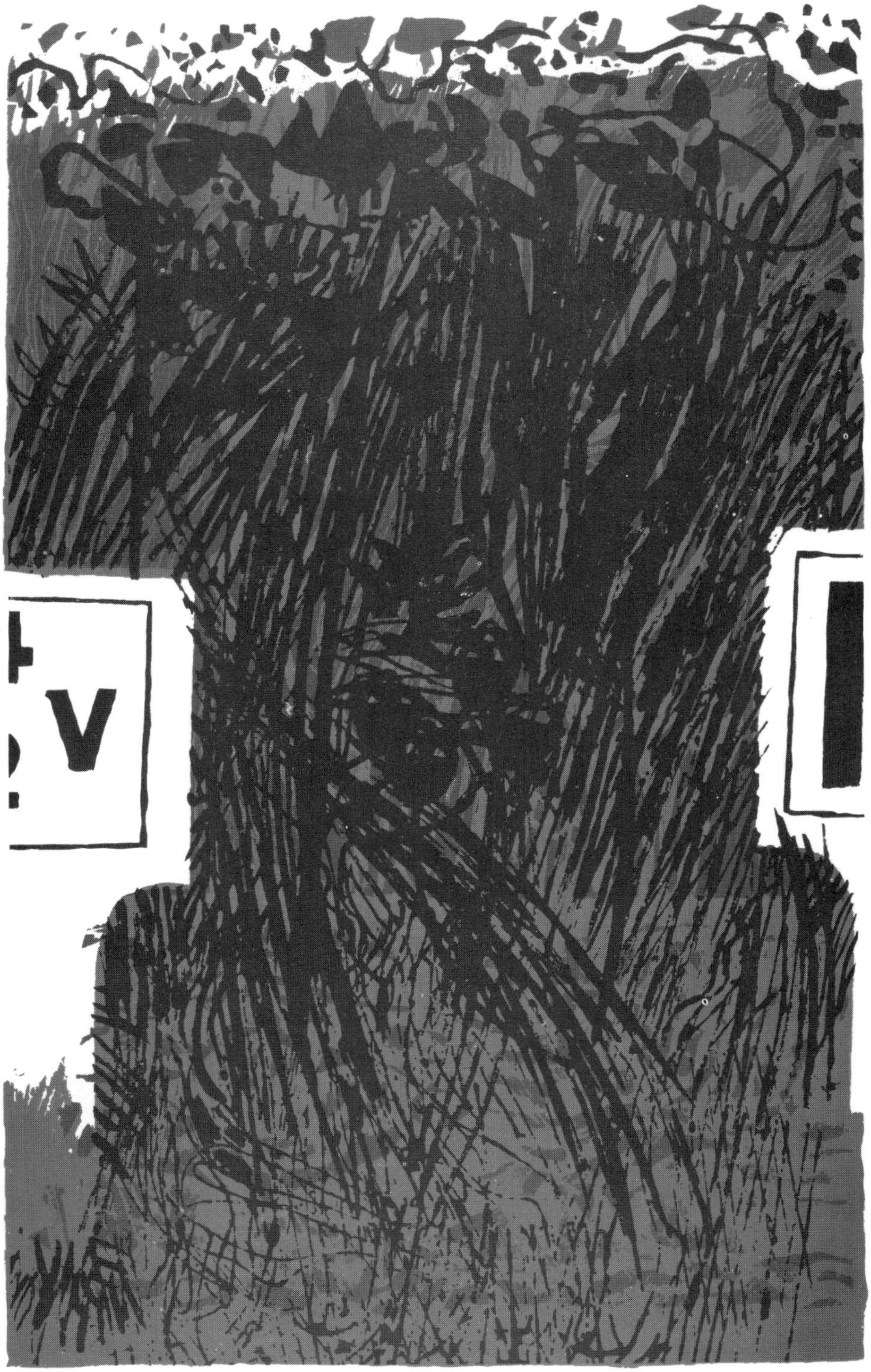

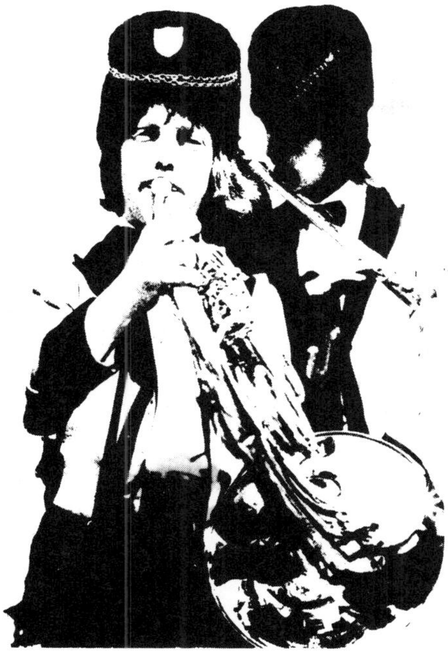

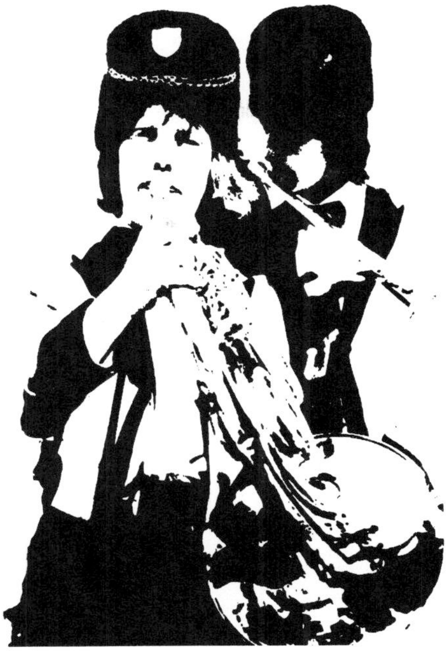

High contrast positive original and print from screen made with sensitised water-based PVA glue. Original positive (*left*). Print (*right*)

different techniques which they then transfer to one screen. Prints from this screen can then be retained for reference.

Just for a start here is a short list of a few of the possibilities:

1 Drawings in soft conte or graphite pencil on tracing paper
2 Paintings in black poster paint on tracing paper
3 Rubbings taken from suitable surfaces in thick black wax crayon
4 Previously printed materials oiled out
5 Semi-translucent actual materials, loosely woven fabrics, etc used either directly or in the form of rubbings
6 Transfer lettering on acetate sheet or tracing paper
7 Photograms made on extra thin photographic paper
8 Collages of old photographic negatives. These will, of course, reproduce as negatives
9 High contrast positives (*Kodaliths*, etc)

Opposite Key drawing made in black paint on tracing paper and transferred to the mesh photographically supporting colour screens produced by working directly onto the mesh

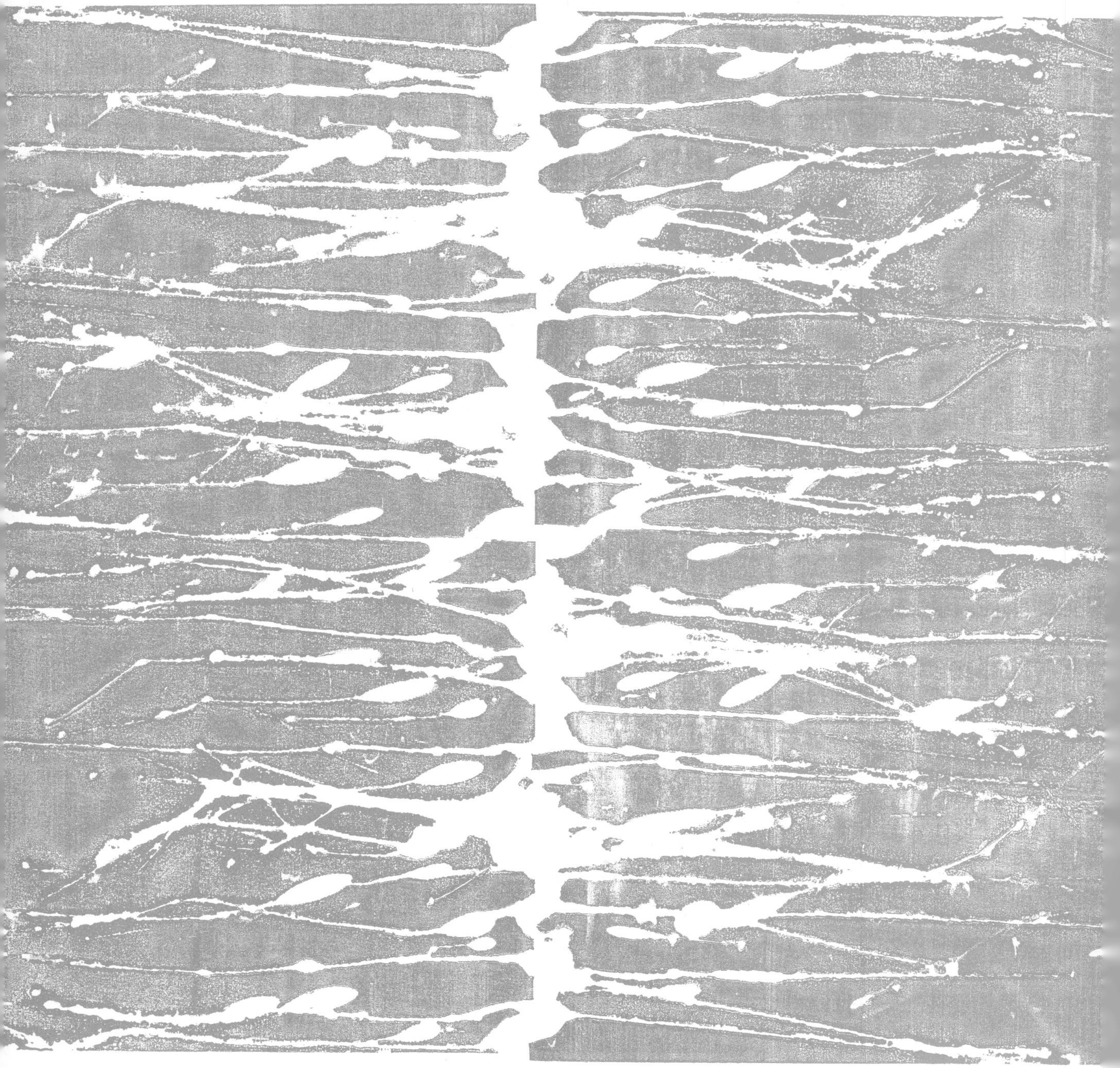

Molten paraffin wax splashed along the top of a screen and allowed to dribble down. An interesting effect is produced by turning the screen and making prints side by side

Printing on fabric and other materials

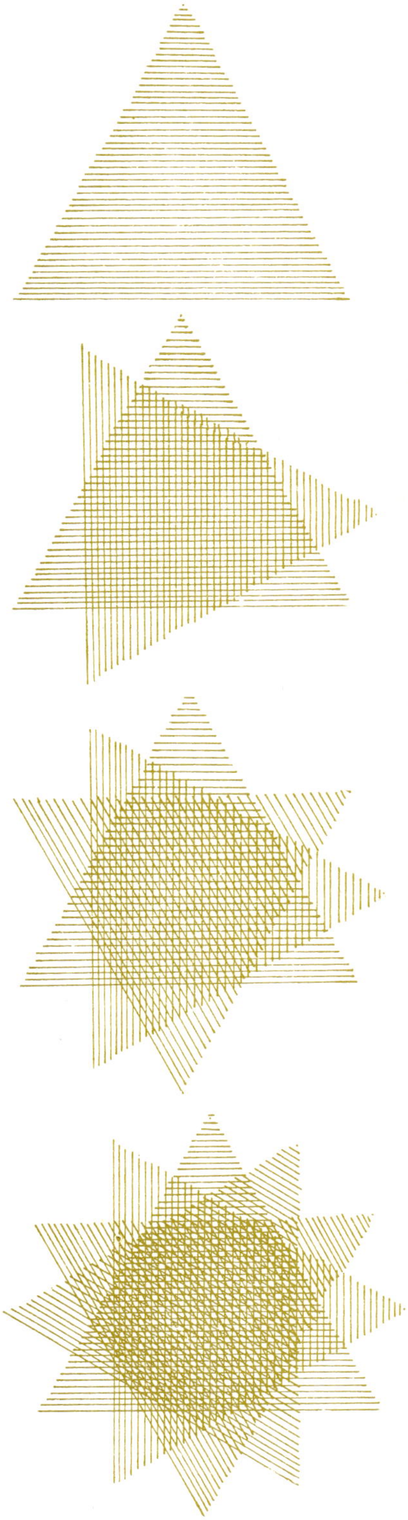

Screen printing is a technique by means of which an image can be created and repeated. In that sense it is simply an instrument of reproduction, and it is this basic aspect of the subject that is the primary concern of this book. All the processes described so far have been related to printmaking on paper for reasons of simplicity. Nevertheless the procedures for producing an image on a screen are very much the same, whether the screen is to be used ultimately for prints, posters, lengths of fabric, wallpapers or even detergent bottles. I am sure many readers will be interested to experiment with printing on cloth.

Fabric printing is, of course, a subject in its own right and there are many excellent books available on the subject (see bibliography). I will limit myself to examining some of the specifically screen printing aspects of fabric printing, and in the process, suggesting one or two approaches which might prove sufficient to start the reader off on a journey into the fascinating world of fabric printing.

First and foremost it must be recognised that most of the dyes and other pigments used in fabric printing are water-based or have water as one of their component ingredients. This means that screens used for fabric printing must be made from stencils which are not water-soluble.

Another major consideration is that when embarking on the printing of a length of fabric, which in itself may be very expensive to purchase, any possibility of the screen failing halfway through must be avoided.

A smudged or spoilt print on paper can simply be discarded, a similar mistake in the middle of a length of fabric constitutes a major disaster. It is advisable, when preparing a screen for fabric printing, to be particularly careful in sealing the inside of the screen with gumstrip and to provide a generous surrounding margin to contain the dye.

Designing a screen which will provide a continuous pattern, without obvious breaks between the individual prints, presents yet another problem for the fabric printer, as does the need to

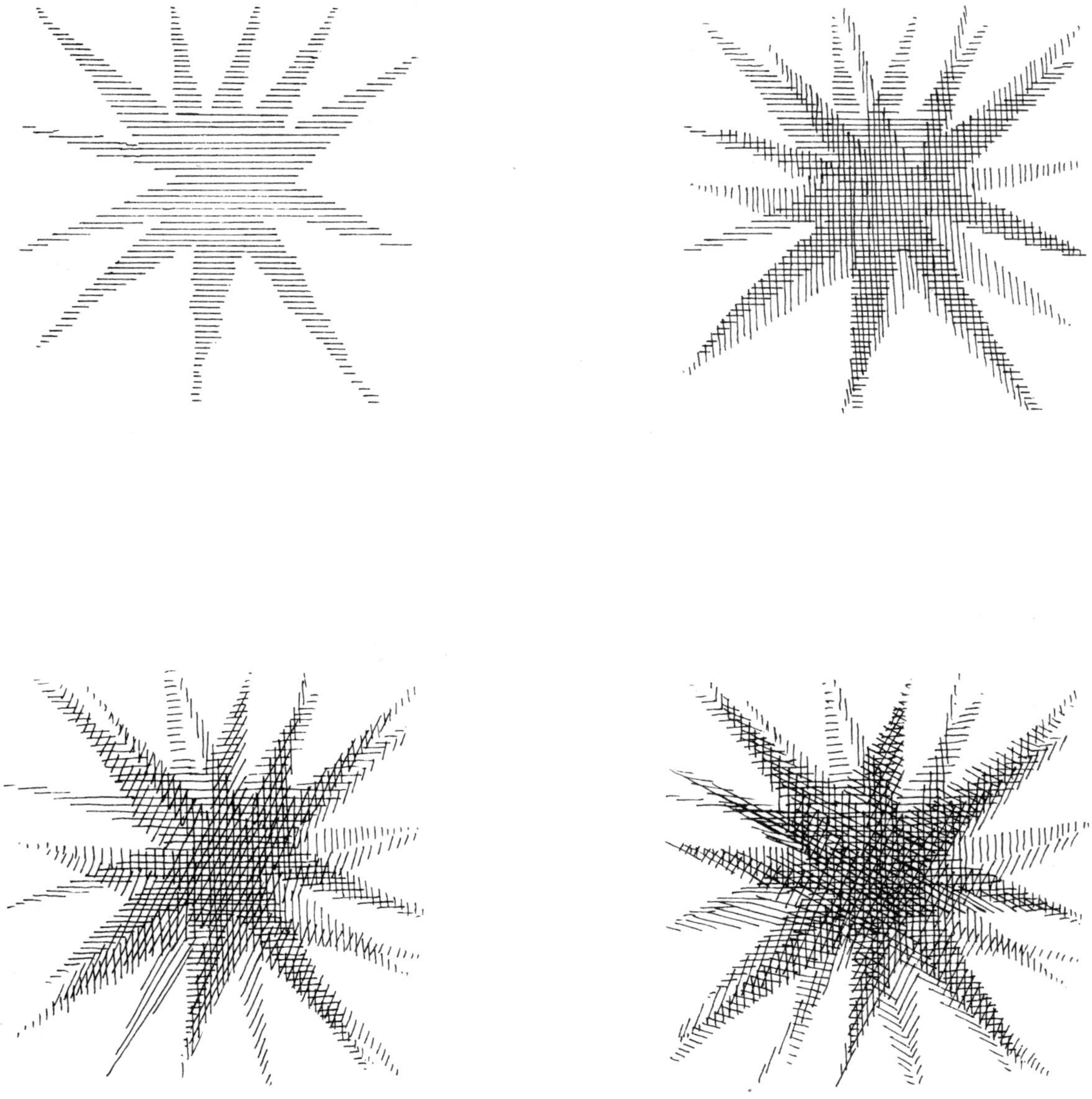

A square screen can be repeatedly turned through 90° and overprinted to produce a rich motif for a fabric print mix sufficient dye of a particular shade to last the whole length of the fabric.

It would probably be advisable for the beginner in screen printing on fabric not to think in terms of lengths of fabric but to concentrate initially, on the production of short lengths such as scarves, squares, place-mats, etc. For a simple experiment, a screen could be prepared with an exactly square 'window'. This can be filled with a design which radiates from the centre, so that at each printing, the screen can be turned through 90°. Thus by very simple means a very rich effect is achieved which will provide the printer with some valuable experience of overprinting on fabric (illustrations pages 67, 68).

It is possible to make use of squares of fabric produced in this way for quite a number of purposes. Possibly the most interesting project involves sewing the squares together to make a patchwork which can be used as a hanging or a bedspread, or as a covering for a room divider. The design can be further enriched by adding some machine embroidery before the squares are sewn together.

Incidentally, readers interested in batik may care to experiment in the use of an open screen as a method of applying dye to a previously waxed fabric.

Overleaf Design created from screens using a variety of techniques including cut paper, gum, wax and PVA

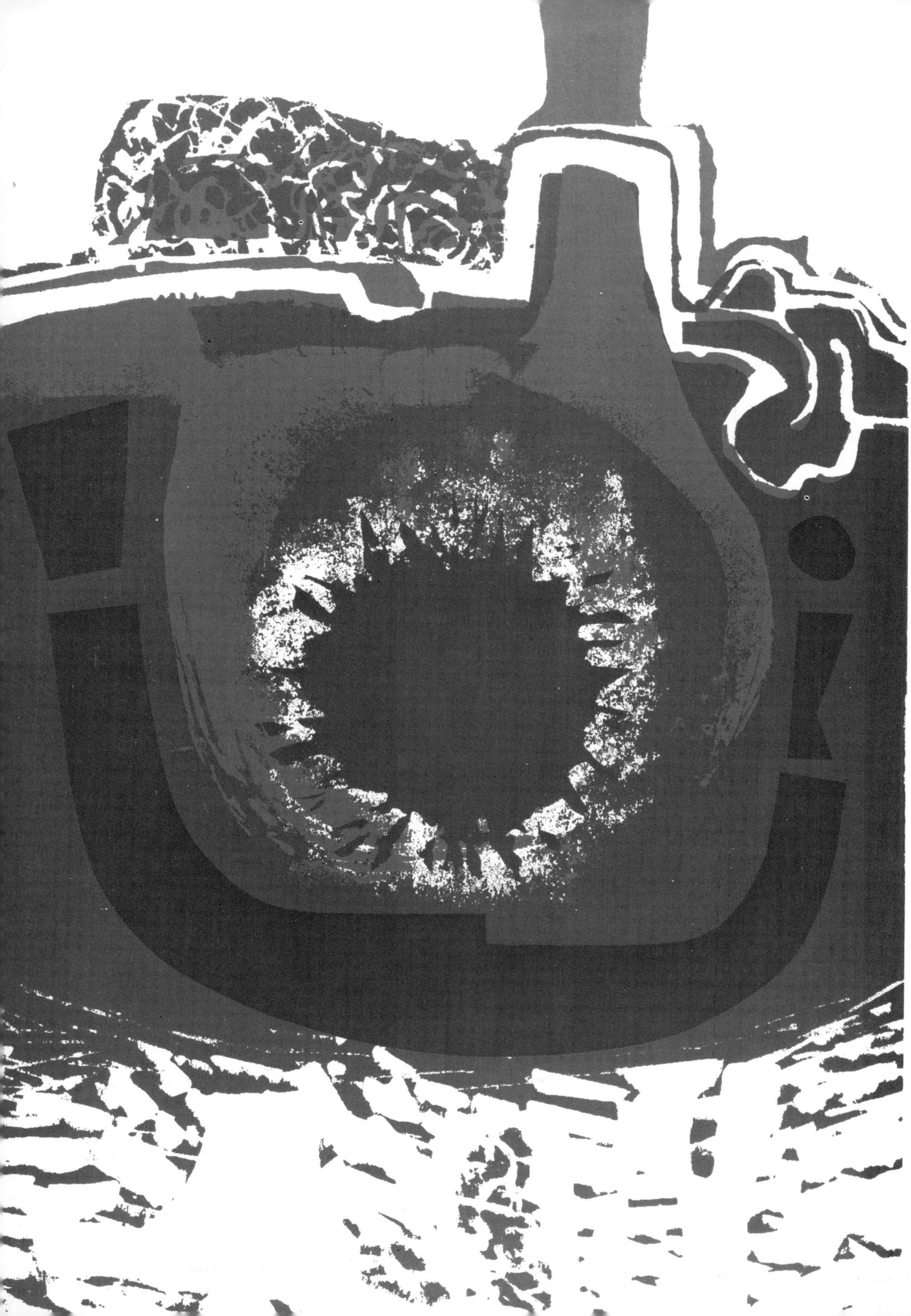

The fabric printing table

The only other item of equipment required specifically by the screen printer working on fabrics is the fabric table. This is a large, flat table top covered by a soft, waterproof overlay. In its most sophisticated form, this overlay is made up of a layer of felt blanket covered by a sheet of rubberised fabric, generally referred to as *Neoprened* sheeting. This product is now very expensive and the reader may wish to find other ways of providing himself with suitable fabric printing surface.

In practice it is possible to put together a very acceptable fabric printing surface, using domestic blanket and the heavy-duty polythene used by builders. A design for a fabric table appears below. The dimensions of the fabric table will largely depend on the character of the work to be done on it. If it is intended to print whole lengths of fabric for use in dressmaking or soft furnishing, the longer the table is the better, in order that one can obtain an uninterrupted run. However for the private individual, there are generally space limitations and a table of about three metres' length is usually adequate for most purposes.

Possibly of greater importance is the width of the table. When printing on fabric it is important to remember that actual width

Fabric printing requires a large, waterproof surface. It also needs to be soft enough to accommodate the screen frame, allowing the stencil to make close contact with the fabric being printed. The longer the table is the better; three metres being about the minimum length desirable. The table should be at least 40 cm wider than the width of the fabric to be printed. Any fabric printing table permanently in position will need to be protected from damage by a hard cover. Table tops which can be stacked away when not in use are a distinct advantage

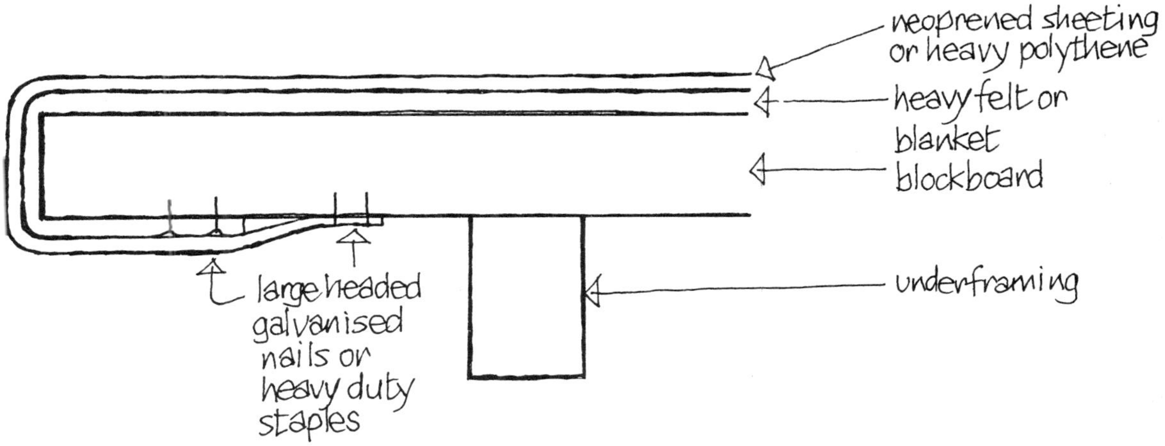

of the printing area can be as little as a half of the total width of the screen, allowing for the masking border, etc. And if the design is to be printed right up to, and possibly over, the selvedge of the material then there must be a considerable width of table extending each side of the fabric to support the screen. It is therefore necessary to construct the table at least 50 cm (20 in.) wider than the widest fabric it is intended to print.

Before the material can be printed it has to be fixed to the table surface. The normal practice is to gum the material to the table using dilute gum and a warm iron. This ensures that there are no creases in the fabric and no shrinkage between the printing of one colour and the next, which would, of course, ruin the registration. Some polythenes, however, do not take kindly to being ironed and when using a polythene covered table it may be advisable simply to fasten the fabric down by the edges with masking or plastic tape. This method is somewhat crude compared with the one employing gum, but provided the design is not too intricate, it generally works reasonably well. It does mean, however, that small areas of fabric remain unprinted along the selvedge, where the tape has been.

One final word of advice on the use of a fabric printing table. The table *must be thoroughly cleaned* before each new length of fabric is fixed into place and it is of equal importance to see that all screens are clean, and dry, before they are used. Care should be taken to protect the table top at all times. Any puncture in the covering will allow dye to penetrate the blanket and this will undoubtedly bleed through and stain the fabric being printed, although to all outward appearances the table is perfectly clean.

Setting out the fabric table

Having produced a design on the screen and having fixed the fabric to the table top, the next task is to mark out the fabric in such a way that the screen can be accurately located for each successive print. It is only in this aspect of the process that the industrial fabric printer has the advantage over his less professional colleague. The industrial printer will possess printing tables fitted with tracks along their length in which the screens will ride. These tracks are in turn fitted with an adjustable notch mechanism which locates the screen very accurately in a predetermied position.

Printers operating below this very professional level will need to mark the positions of the screen on the fabric itself. The first job is to mark the limits of the printed area on the outside of the screen frame and relate this to a square or a rectangle which can be indicated on the fabric itself. This is done by using two weighted lines of fine string coated with tailor's chalk. The lines are 'pinged' or 'snapped' into position and when removed leave a fine chalk line against which the marks on the outside of the screen can set (see illustration page 74). The chalk lines will subsequently brush or wash out of the fabric. Incidentally, in marking out the screen it must not be assumed that the frame is square and a set-square should always be employed to establish the limits of the repeat.

When producing a multi-coloured fabric each successive screen must, of course, be closely matched one with another in terms of marking-out if precise overprinting is to be achieved. It must be remembered that even with the most accurately marked screens, it is almost impossible to print one long, straight edge of dye against another without either overlapping or leaving a fine gap. In either case the fabric is spoiled and the answer, as suggested previously, is to avoid creating designs in which this is likely to happen.

It is also a good plan to adopt a printing procedure in which one progresses along the fabric printing only every other square, returning to the beginning to complete the pattern after the first prints are dry. If this procedure is followed there is no danger of picking up wet dye on the underside of the screen frame and soiling the fabric.

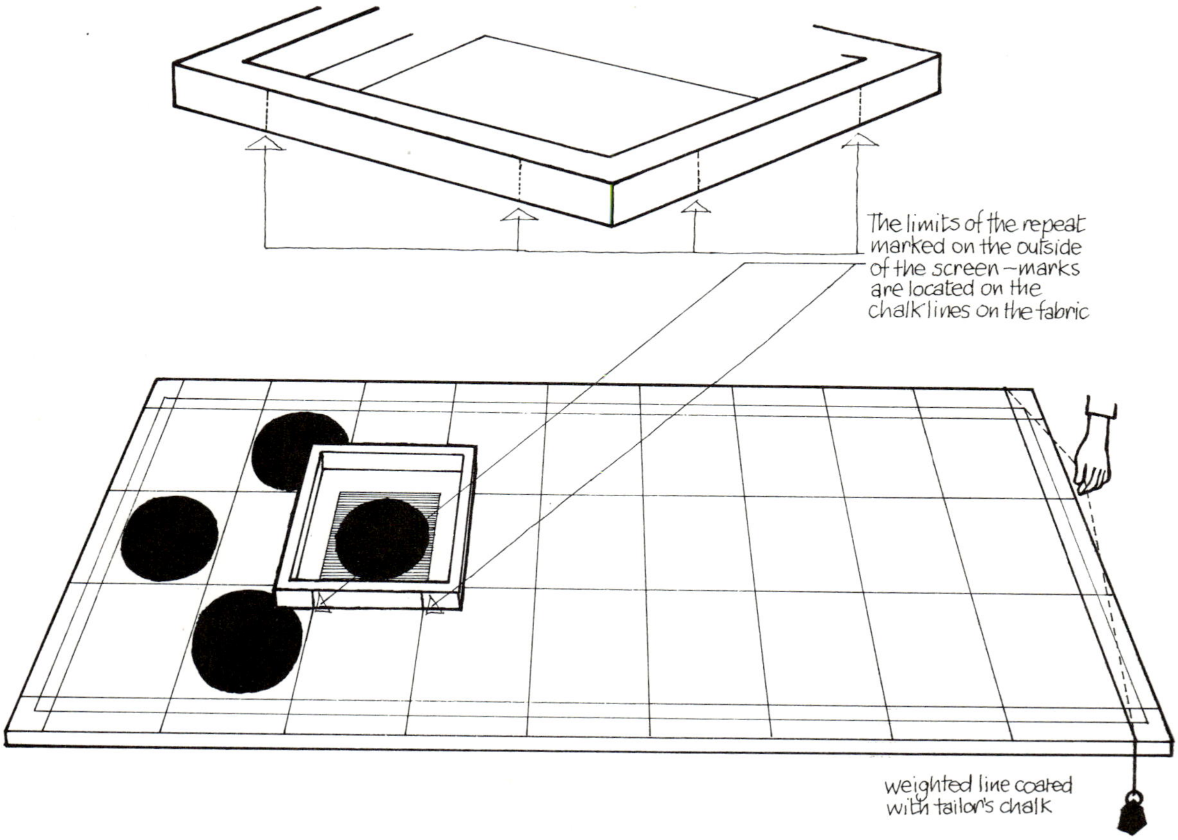

The fabric is fixed to the table, preferably by ironing down with gum, although in certain circumstances the edge of the fabric can be held down by masking strip or *Sellotape*. A grid corresponding to the printing area of the stencil is marked on the fabric by using a line coated with tailor's chalk which is 'pinged' on to the fabric at the appropriate intervals. It is advisable to stagger the printing as shown in the diagram to avoid any possibility of the screen frame smudging the previous wet prints

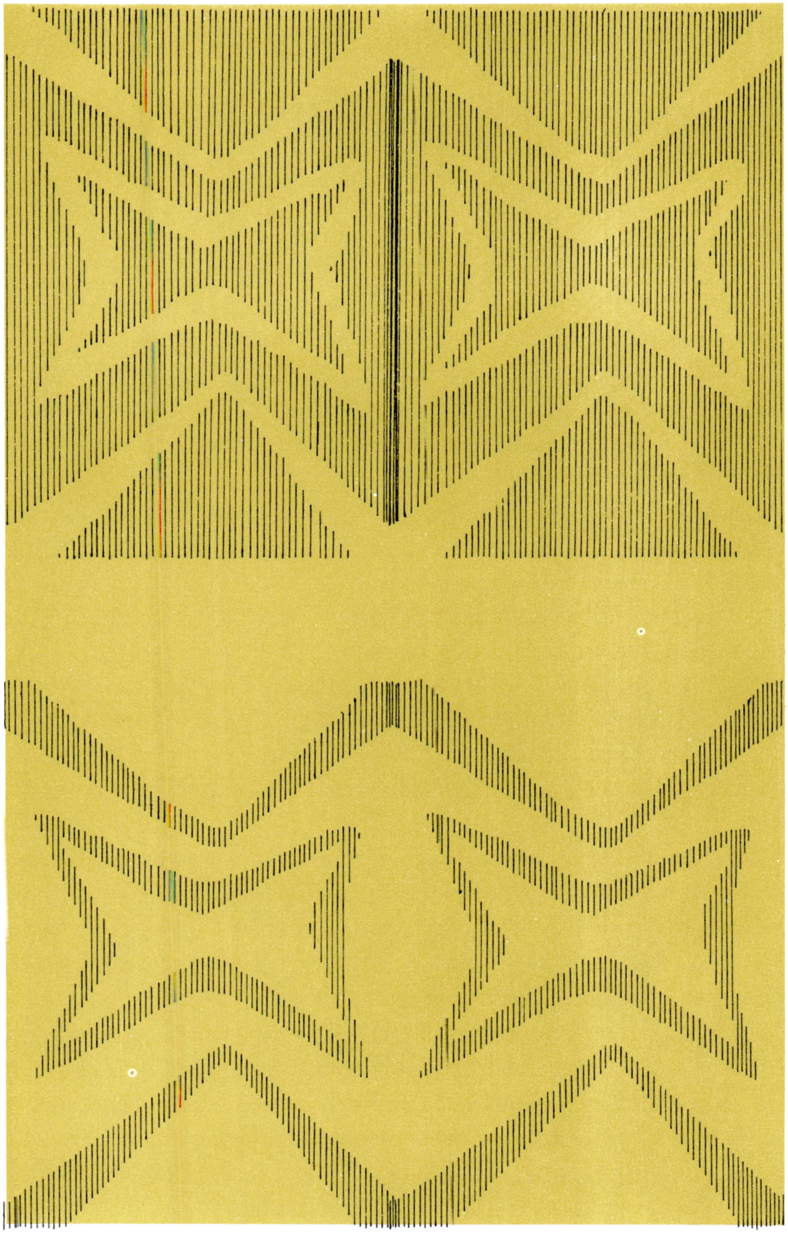

As far as possible a fabric repeat should be designed to avoid the need to butt up long straight edges of colour against each other. One needs considerable skill and quite sophisticated equipment to avoid either an overlap (as shown in this diagram) or a narrow gap. In both cases the errors will be most obtrusive in the final printed fabric

Where the joining areas are only small or can be incorporated into the design, any slight inaccuracies in the printing will be much less noticeable

Designing a 'repeat'

Producing a fabric or wallpaper design which can be printed in units (screens) but which finally gives the effect of a continuous all-over pattern requires considerable skill and experience. Any reader who has studied the block prints of William Morris with a view to discovering where one unit ended and another began will understand the problem.

As I mentioned earlier there are many books available on the subject of fabric design which deal with this problem in some detail. There are, however, two points that are worth making at this stage which may help the reader when he or she comes to mark out a fabric for screen printing.

1 Any screen which is designed to print contiguous to itself should under no circumstances have large open (that is printed) areas at its edge, either at the top and bottom, or at the sides. This is, perhaps, best explained by reference to the diagram on page 75.

2 Where possible the design should be transferred to the screen in such a way that it does not sit neatly in the middle of the screen. If the image can conveniently be halved or even quartered and, as it were, spread around the screen then a more overall, continuous effect can be achieved.

It must also be remembered that even a medium sized screen will be a much larger printing unit than is available in any other fabric printing technique and can be designed to accommodate a number of identical motifs which can be all printed together in one go. This is particularly convenient when producing the design on the screen by photographic means.

Preliminary experiments

All the chapters in this book have up to this point been concerned with describing the basic equipment required for screen printing and outlining the elementary procedures. Before proceeding further it would be appropriate for the reader to conduct some simple experiments in order to familiarise himself with the 'feel' of the process so that he can begin to design 'through' the medium as well as for the medium.

Overleaf Texture screen prints produced by rubbings. Rubbings in wax directly on to the mesh, printed in water-based pigment (*left*). The same screen coated with gum, the wax removed and the screen printed in oil-based ink (*right*)

Screen printing is such a versatile medium that it will accommodate a very wide range of different approaches to design, and as with any other creative craft characteristic images can be evolved which could not easily be produced by any other medium.

One of the most fascinating aspects of screen printing is the number of effects that can be discovered during one's exploration of the medium, some of which may be arrived at by accident but which can be developed and exploited in a more controlled fashion later.

There are many difficulties facing the author of a book which sets out to describe a printing process. Perhaps one of the most pressing is the problem of avoiding the giving of advice on image making as distinct from advice on the technical aspects of the subject. In a book of this nature it is impossible to even touch on the very difficult matter of aesthetics.

One piece of advice, however, I do feel must be offered. I believe it would be a mistake for the reader to concern himself with any attempt at representational picture-making whilst conducting his first experiments in screen printing. It would be far better in the early stages to concentrate on simple non-figurative images as a foundation for the exploration of basic techniques.

Virtually any substance or material which will prevent the pigment from passing through the mesh of the screen without, at the same time, obstructing the passage of the squeegee can be used as a screen stencil. It is possible to make use of a material such as thin paper, which can be stuck to the mesh with adhesive

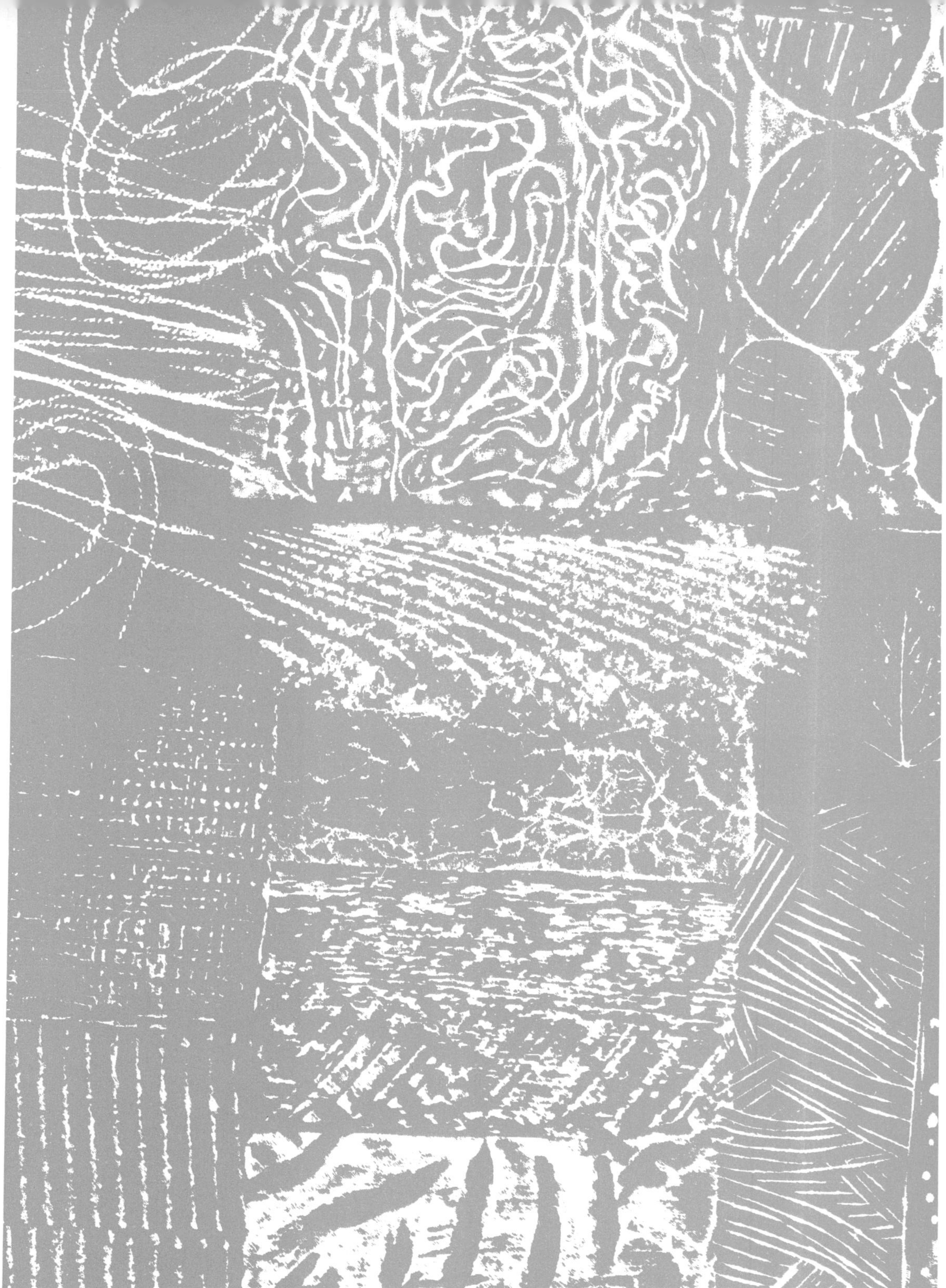

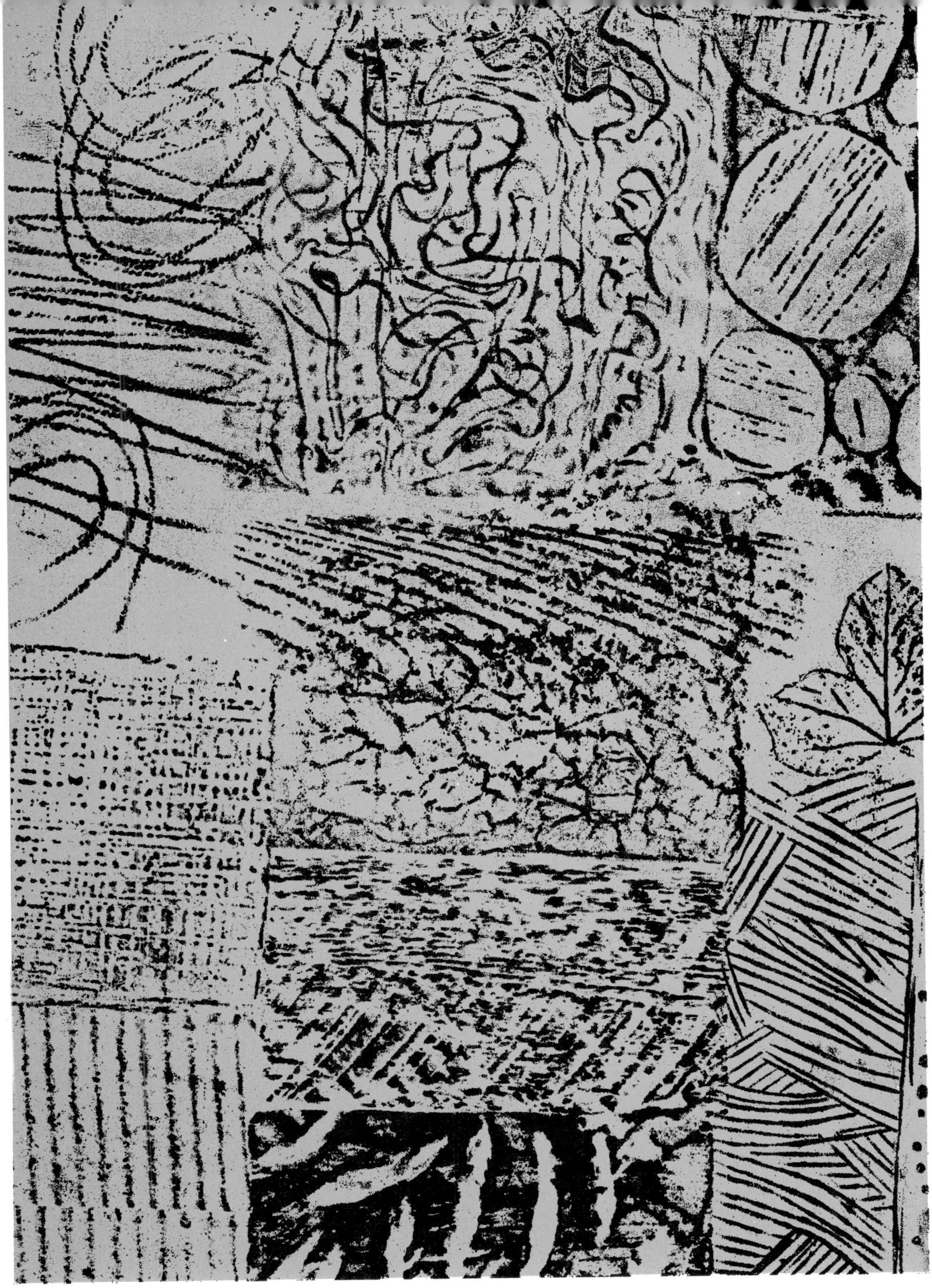

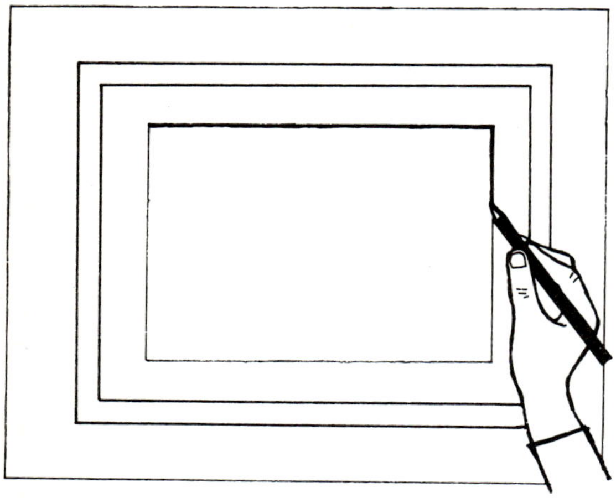

(a)

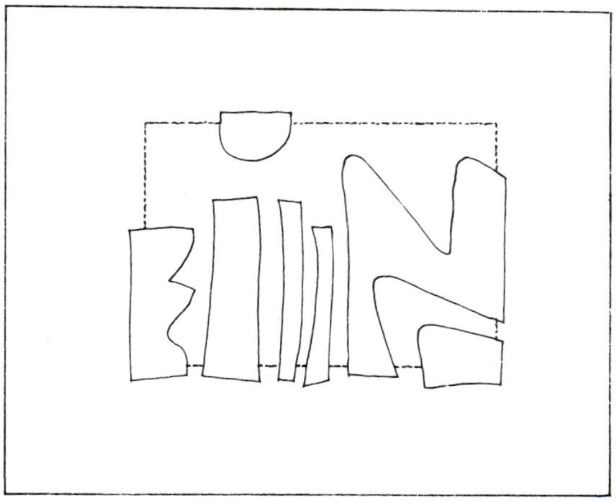

(b)

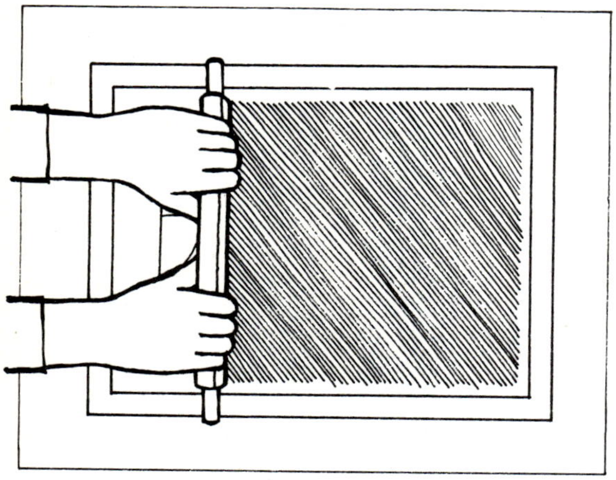

(c)

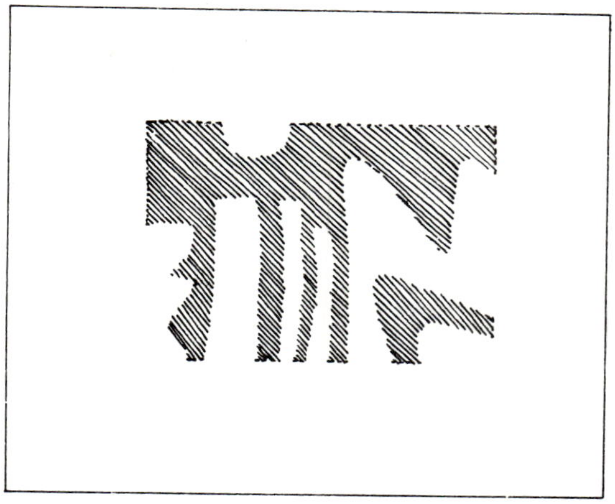

(d)

(a) Marking the perimeter of the rectangle to be printed through the mesh with a soft pencil or stick of charcoal
(b) Cut-out newsprint shapes placed on the marked area ready to be picked up by the screen
(c) The pigment is squeegeed across the screen fixing the newsprint shapes to the work
(d) The printed design which remains when the screen has been removed

or a liquid substance which can be painted on to the mesh and allowed to dry. It is also possible to achieve a partial blocking of the screen by rubbing wax or some other appropriate dry substance into the mesh.

Probably the easiest and most direct results can be obtained by making the stencil from newsprint. Ordinary printed newspaper will do, but for really clean prints, use plain newsprint, thin, neutral coloured sugar paper or white lining paper. Under no circumstances should any attempt be made to make paper stencils from cartridge paper or any other heavy, good quality paper.

For the first experiment, a pile of printing paper of a

convenient size should be set out on the printing table. The masked screen should be located on the top sheet and the corners of the printing area marked through the mesh with a soft pencil. When the screen is removed, the corners can be joined by a line which will delineate the outside shape of the final printed image.

Some newsprint shapes can be arranged to form a design inside this marked area. None of these shapes should be larger than about a quarter of the total area or smaller than about one inch in its smallest dimension. The screen can now be replaced over this arrangement using the open area of the mesh as a kind of window. Pigment can now be applied to the screen and the printing procedure previously described can be followed. The first pull with the squeegee will pick up the paper shapes which will then remain attached to the mesh whilst subsequent prints are made. When a change of design or colour is required, the shapes can easily be removed and the screen cleaned down. Of course it is inadvisable to allow the pigment to dry behind the paper stencil as the pigment will, in effect, glue the paper to the mesh not only making the removal of the paper difficult but also causing the mesh to become blocked with pigment. Should this happen there is generally an appropriate solvent which will soften the pigment and allow the screen to be cleaned, but it entails one extra chore.

Once the screen is clean and dry, a fresh stencil can be prepared from another group of paper shapes, arranged on one of the first set of prints and a second colour applied. In this way some substantial experience of multi-coloured screen printing can be gained with the minimum of technical means.

A more controlled and permanent version of this method can be achieved by cutting the shapes in gummed paper and sticking them directly to the screen mesh. More effort is needed to remove the gummed paper and if this method is used it might be advisable to apply the second colour with a second screen.

Should there be a need to change the colour of the pigment without changing the stencil shapes the screen can be placed on a pad of old newspapers and the bulk of the previous pigment removed with a palette knife or spoon. A square-ended palette knife is a most useful instrument for this purpose and can be made by filing a palette or old kitchen knife square (see illustration page 21). Having cleared away the bulk of the old pigment in this fashion, the rest can be removed with a rag or dry sponge. There are limits to the efficiency of this method and if it

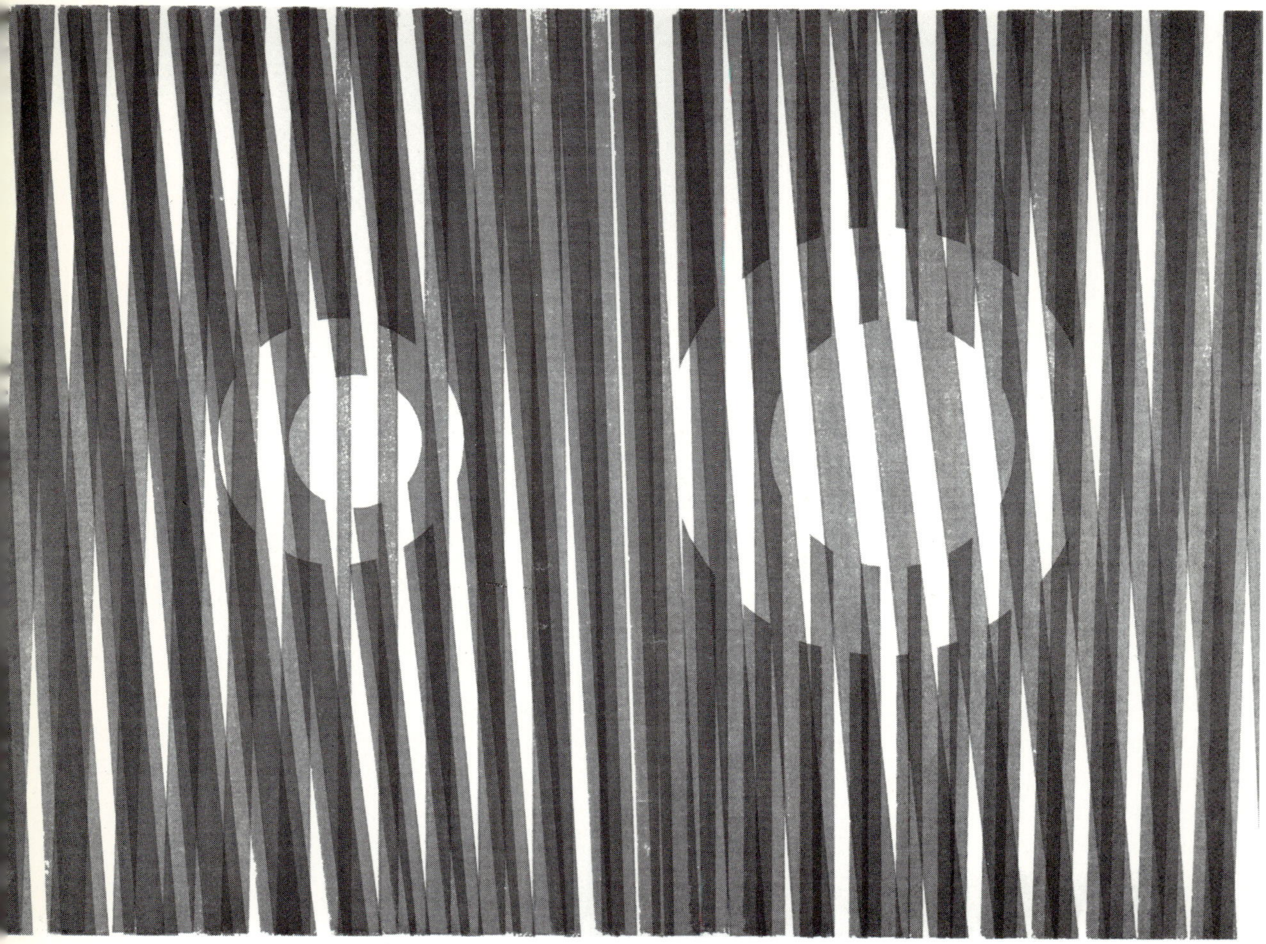

Direct stencil: cut paper and transparent adhesive tape printed in oil-based inks using extender base

is intended to use a sequence of colours with the same stencil it is advisable to follow the good printmaking practice of commencing with the lightest colour and working through to the darkest or strongest. It would not be sensible to begin with black or dark red and attempt to follow such a colour with yellow.

The paper stencil technique is by far the simplest and most direct method of producing a stencil on a screen; it is ideal for early experiments but it has severe limitations from the design point of view. Using a paper stencil, it is almost impossible to achieve line or texture effects and the beginner will soon experience the need for techniques which will extend the range of possibilities open to him.

Designs of a more linear character can be created by painting

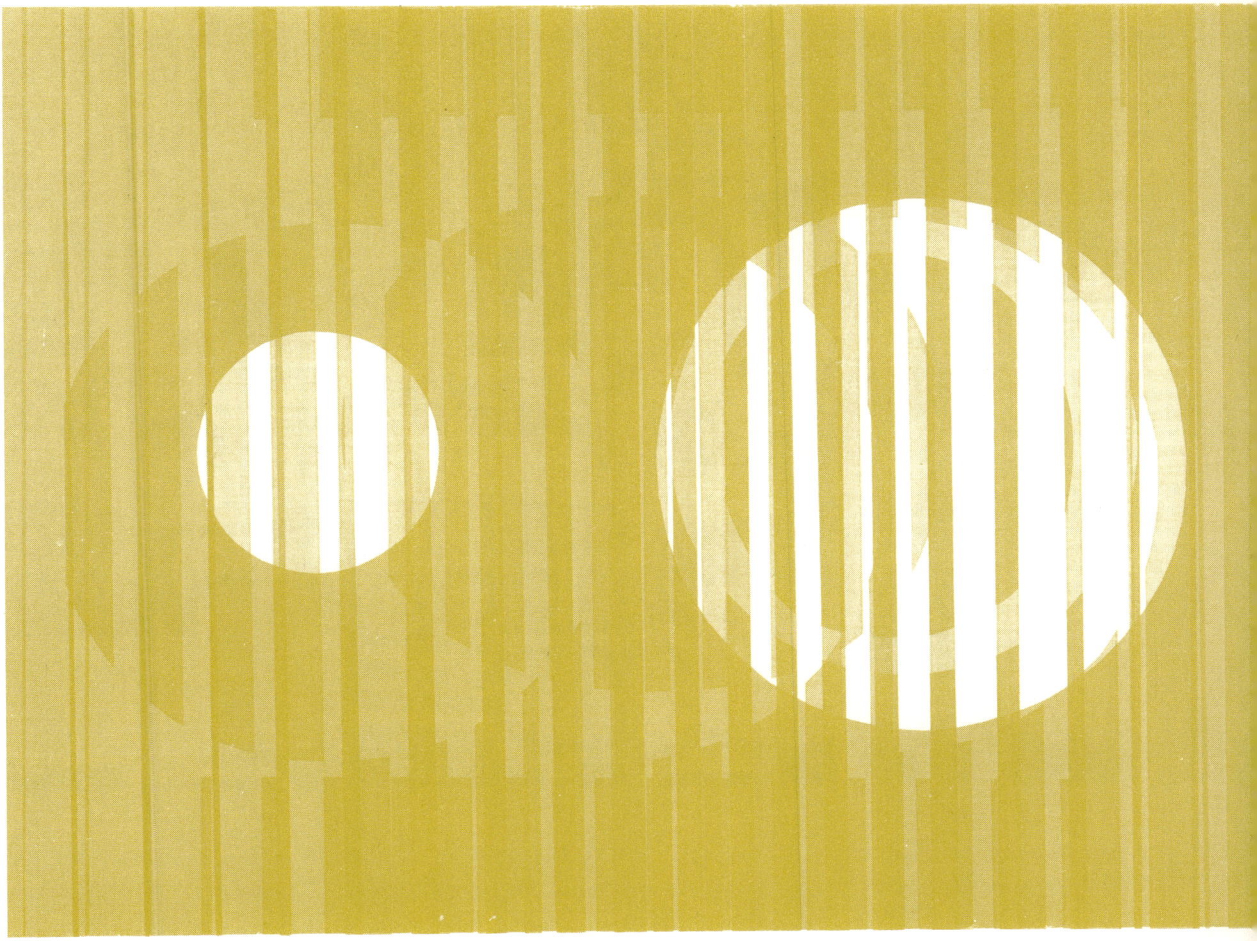

Direct stencil: cut paper and transparent adhesive tape printed in oil-based inks using transparent extender base

the mesh with one or another of a number of liquid substances which, once dry, will not re-dissolve or be broken down by the medium in which the design is to be printed. Lacquer, oil paint, plastic emulsion paint (PVA), starch paste, french polish, proprietary screen fillers, glues and gums, paraffin wax etc. can all be used in one form or another, depending on the characteristics of the pigment to be used for the print.

For the first experiments, paraffin wax is a most useful medium since it dries – or more accurately sets – almost immediately, so that the screen is at once ready for use. Wax is also very easily removed from the mesh when a change of design is required.

Paraffin wax – the kind used for the manufacture of candles –

A lacquer screen worked on progressively, adding more lacquer after the printing of each colour

is normally solid and has to be melted down before it can be painted or dribbled on to the mesh. There are techniques in which solid wax is used and these will be described later.

Wax should be melted in a water-jacket or glue-pot and never by direct heat. In the absence of a proper glue-pot, the wax can be contained in an old tin can which in turn, is stood in a saucepan of water over the heating element. Provided the water is not allowed to evaporate, the wax will never reach a temperature at which it will give off noxious and inflammable fumes. Although candles can be used as a source of wax it is better if possible, to make use of pure paraffin wax which has a very low melting point. Modern candles contain unwelcome impurities and are also more difficult to melt.

Once the wax has been reduced to a liquid it can be painted, dribbled, splashed or spattered on to the mesh rather in the manner of a fabric artist working in batik. Indeed because of the similarity of the two techniques it is possible to produce a screen which, when printed, will imitate the effect of batik very closely. The molten wax sets very quickly once it is removed from the heat so speed is needed when applying it to the mesh, and solid blobs of wax should be avoided as these will cause the squeegee to 'jump' during the printing. Any unnecessarily thick areas of wax can be removed by gentle scraping with a wooden spatula or plastic knife, whilst supporting the other side of the mesh with the palm of the hand.

A wax stencil will survive quite a long printing run with a water-based pigment. However the wax is fairly soluble in mineral spirit so that, on the whole, the use of spirit based inks is not recommended with a wax stencil.

To remove the wax at the end of the printing run, all traces of pigment must be removed and the mesh heated between sheets of old newspaper with a hot domestic iron. Wax can also be removed from the screen by flooding it with very hot water in a sink. If this method is employed the drain plug should be left in to prevent the wax-filled water getting into the drainage system. If the water in the sink is allowed to cool the re-hardened wax will float to the top of the water and can be reclaimed for further use.

Wax is a medium which can be changed and developed during the course of a particular printing run. It is easy to add wax to the stencil before printing with another colour; it is also possible to remove wax selectively by putting the screen down on a pad of newspaper and drawing into the wax with an electric soldering iron. The iron can be held in place just long enough to melt the wax so that it runs into the newspaper, but not so long that it damages the mesh.

It was suggested earlier that solid wax could be used as a medium under certain circumstances. A screen mesh can be placed over a suitable textured surface and solid wax applied very much in the same way as one would make a rubbing from an old church brass. With any luck a fair representation of the surface will be transferred to the mesh in wax.

It must be admitted that wax can only be used to produce fairly coarse images. Many other substances, of the kind referred to earlier, lend themselves to more delicate work and should be experimented with. It is also possible to use a number of different media on the same screen, but care must be taken to observe the rules relating to solubility, in connection with the particular medium to be used for printing and in connection with substances employed to clean the screen.

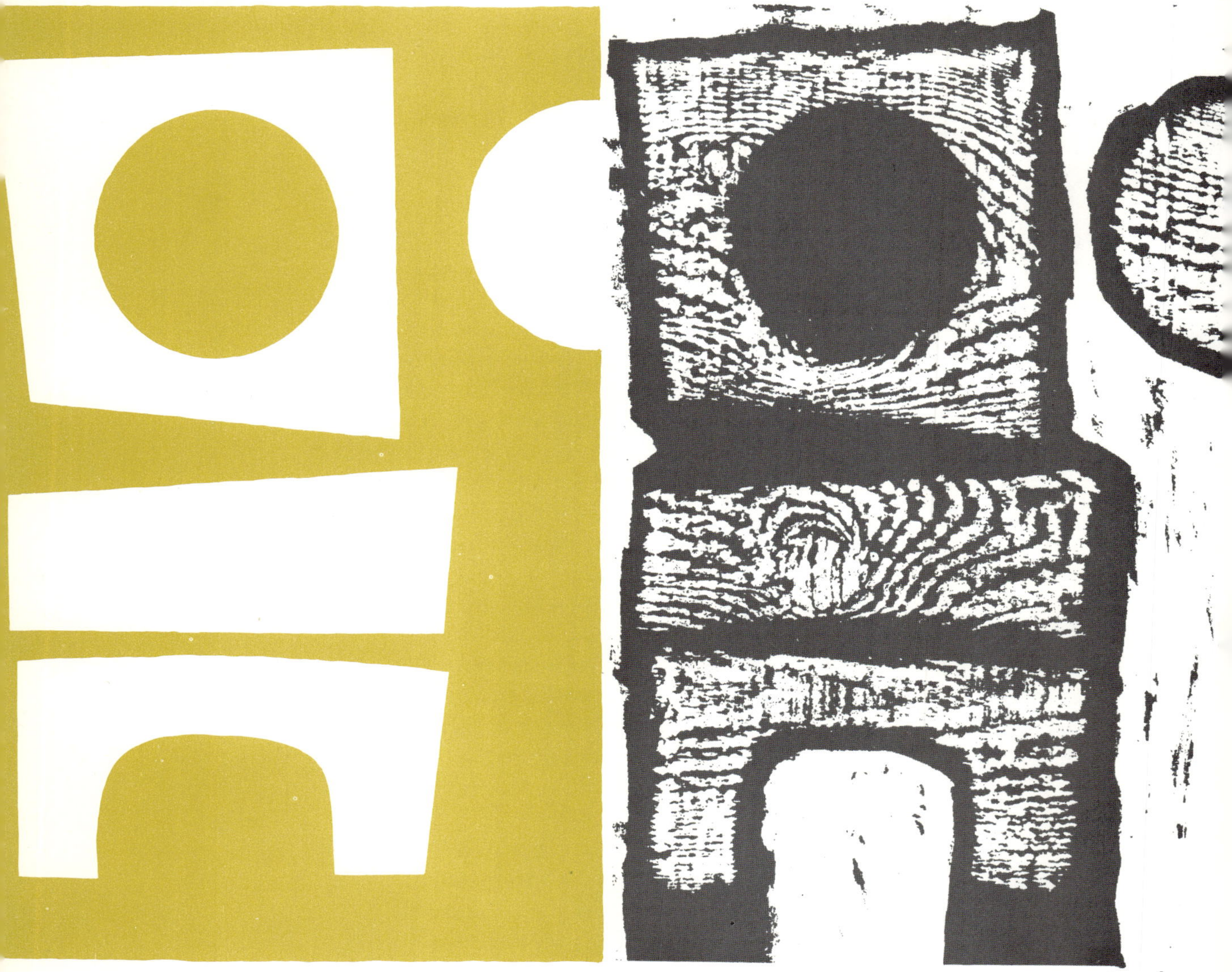

Prints were made from a cut paper 'pick-up' screen. The paper shapes were removed and the screen cleaned. Wax rubbings from grainy timber were made directly on to the organdie in the spaces where the paper shapes had been. The side areas were filled with molten wax and a second colour printed

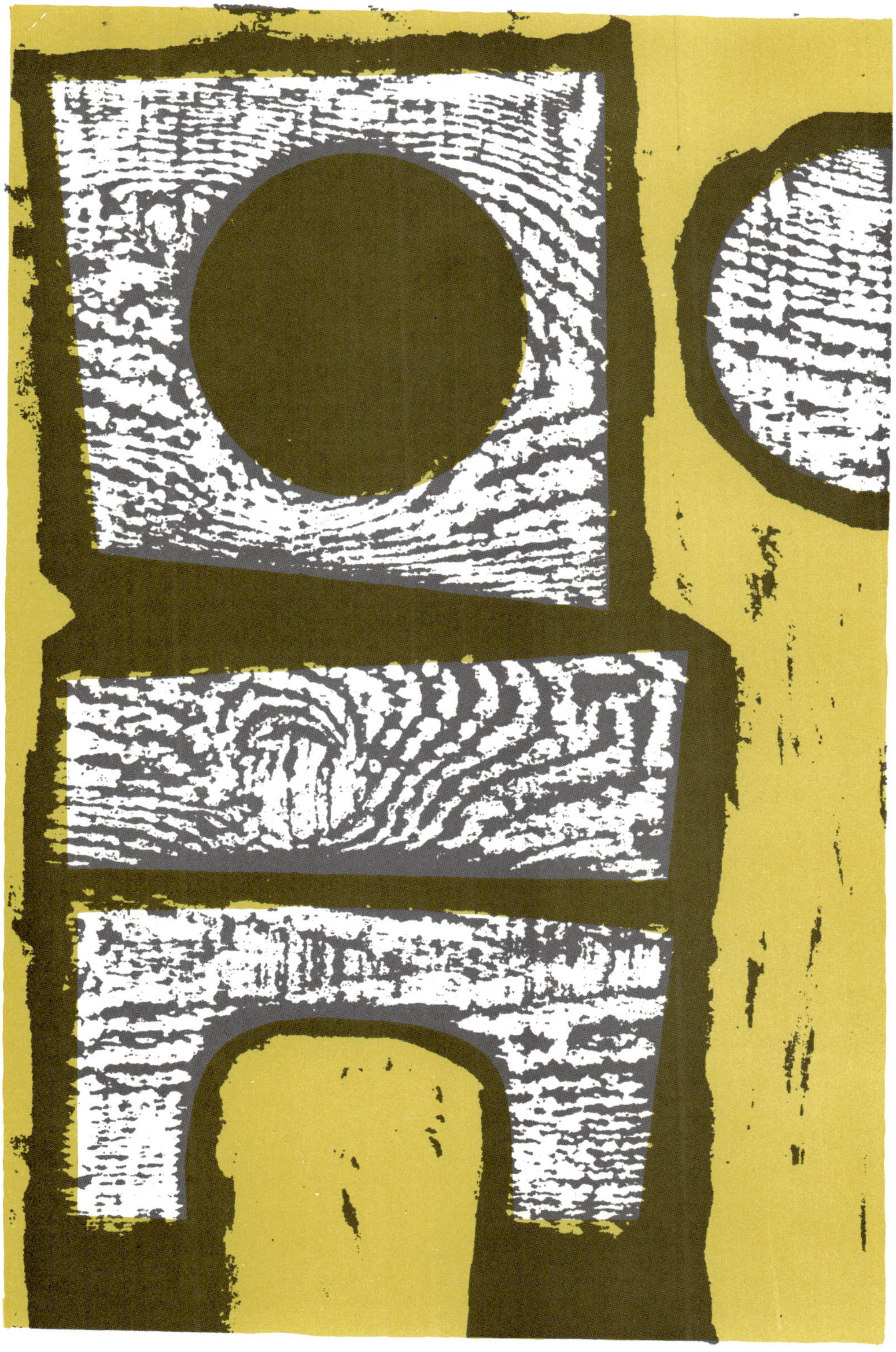

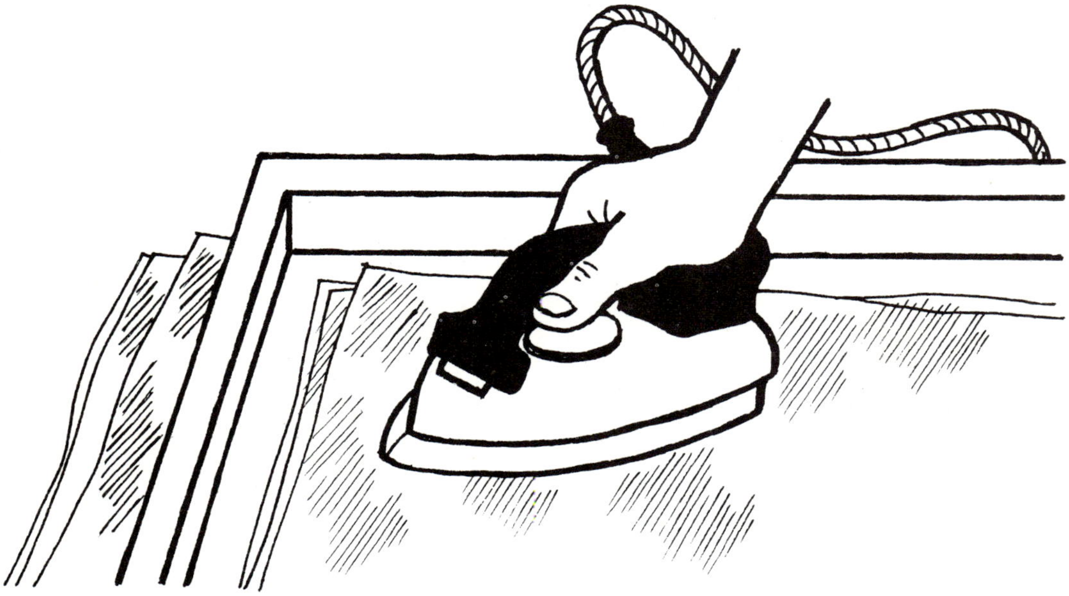

Wax removed by
ironing between pads of
newspaper. With thick wax,
the newspaper should be
changed, or at least turned
around, from time to time

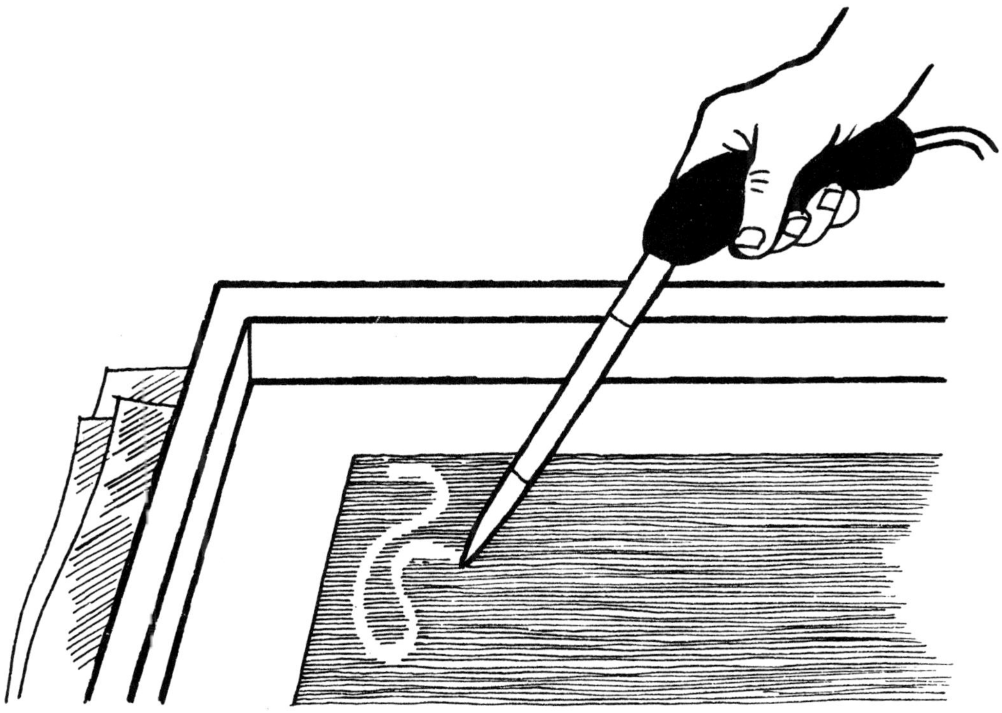

Wax removed in a controlled way with an electric soldering iron

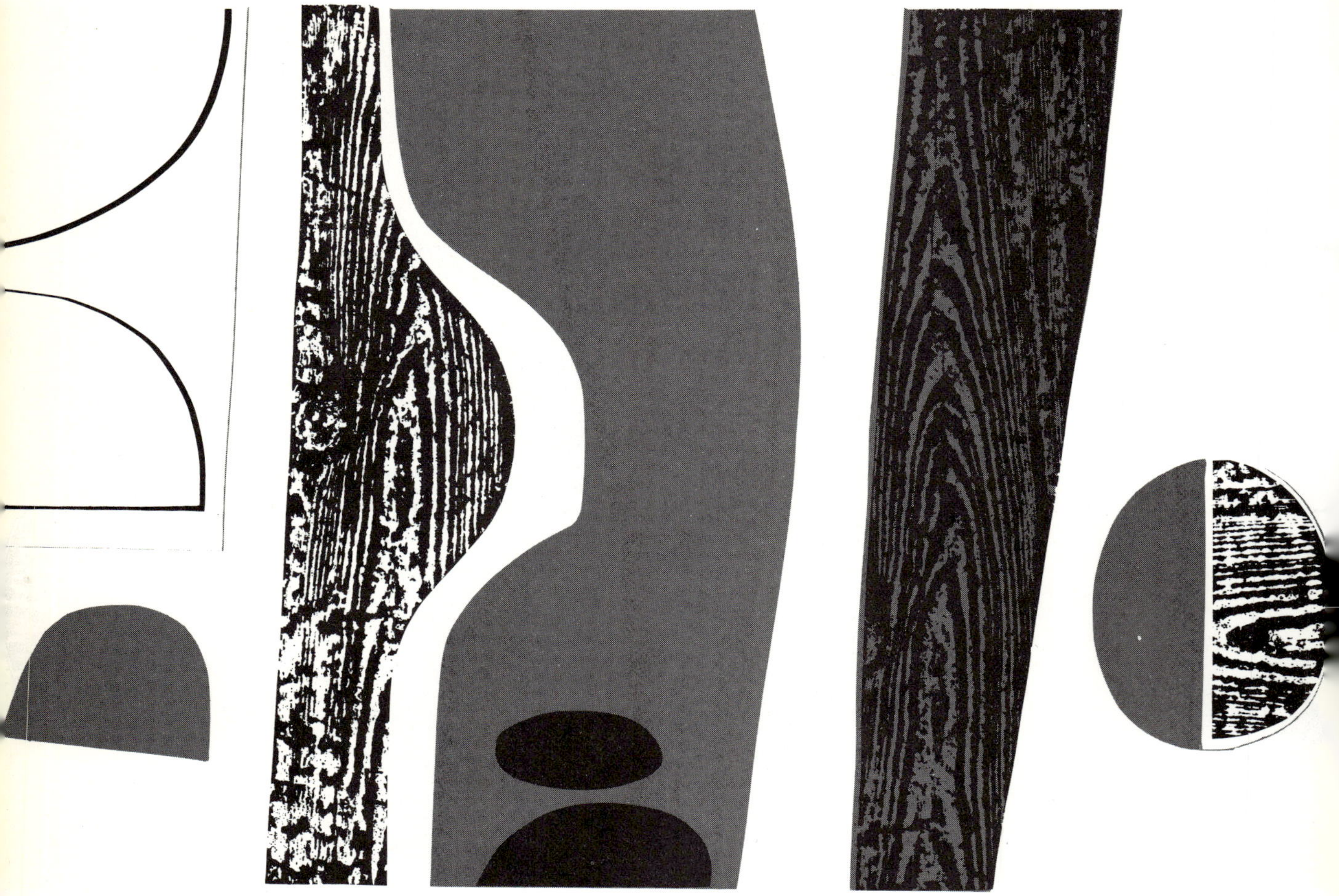

Direct stencil. Wax rubbings
gummed out and cut paper

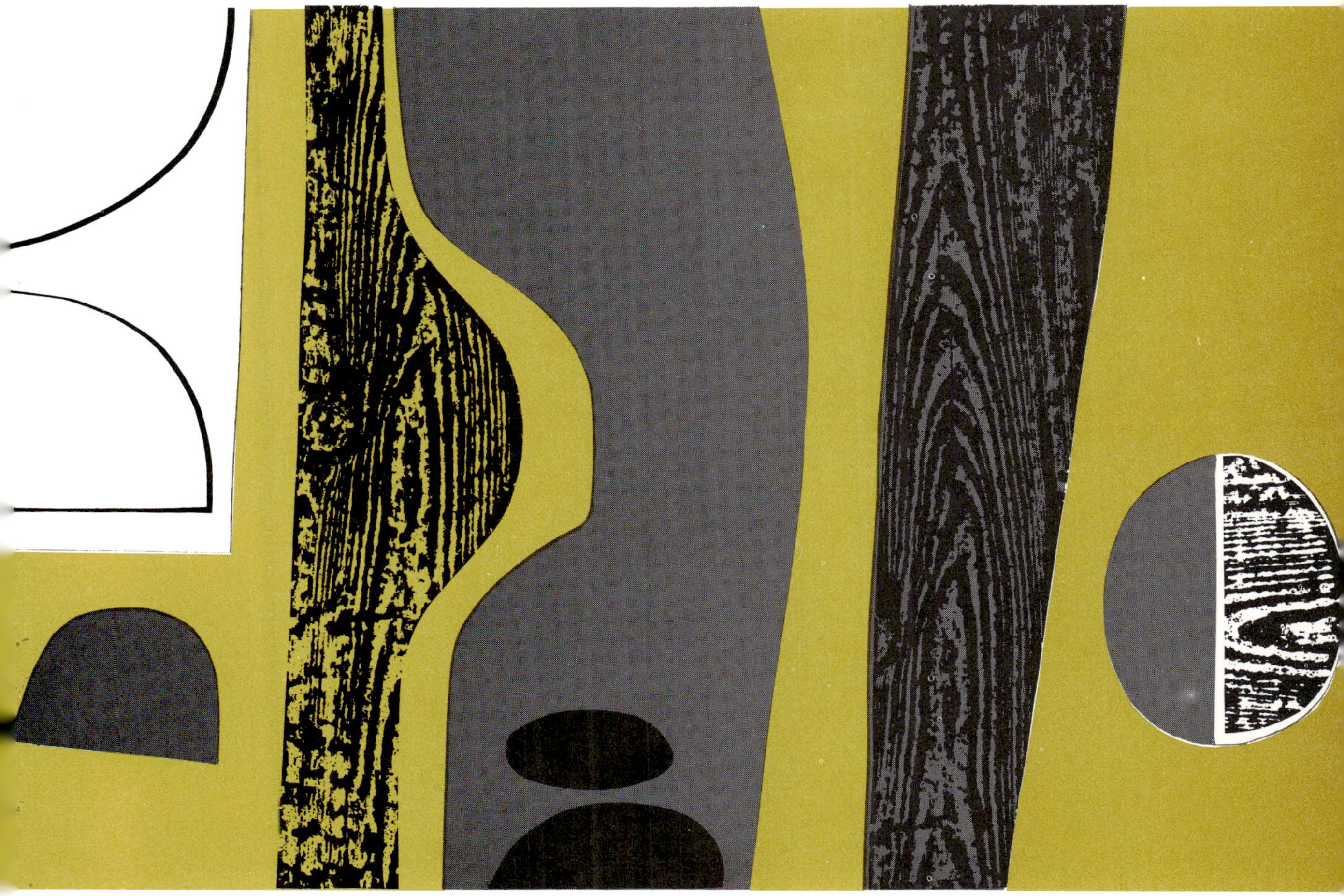

Direct stencil. Wax rubbings gummed out and cut paper

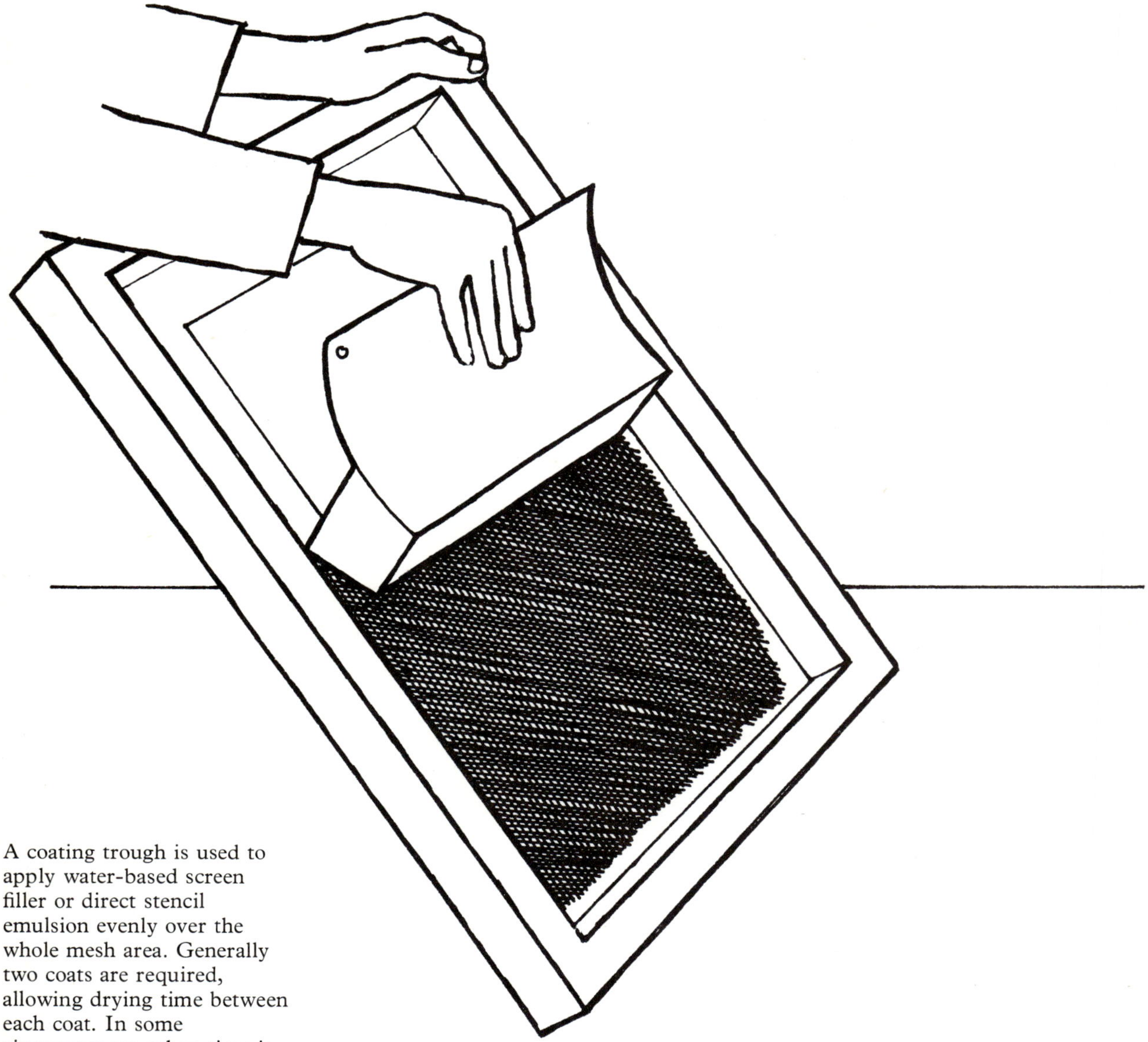

A coating trough is used to apply water-based screen filler or direct stencil emulsion evenly over the whole mesh area. Generally two coats are required, allowing drying time between each coat. In some circumstances, when time is short, it is possible to manage with only one coating but inevitably a certain amount of retouching will be required to eliminate 'pin-holes'. In the absence of a coating trough a squeegee or a strip of hardboard or masonite can be used to coat the mesh, but it is useless to try to apply an even coating with an ordinary paint brush

Producing a positive image

Both the techniques described previously produce what could be described as a 'negative' image on the screen. In other words the marks made on the mesh result in a stencil which reproduces those marks in white on black (or whatever colour pigment happens to be used). Obviously it is quite possible to reproduce a design positively by laboriously painting round the required shapes, rather in the way Victorian wood engravers reproduced pen drawings by cutting away the wood each side of the line. This, however, is a laborious process.

The definitive method for producing a screen which positively reproduces an existing image involves the creation of a stencil photographically, and this process will be described in detail later in the book. For the beginner there are a number of simple ways of making a positive stencil, including the use of wax. A design is created on the mesh in wax as before, but instead of printing the screen, the mesh is coated all over with a water-based material such as glue, gelatine, PVA, etc. When this coating is thoroughly dry, the wax, which has resisted the water-based material, can be removed from the mesh by ironing, leaving an open screen in its place. The printed screen will exactly reproduce the original wax image.

Care must be exercised when removing the wax not to scorch or damage the coating and obviously no substance should be used to remove the wax which will also remove the coating. There are a number of petroleum-based solvents which will remove the wax if removal by heat is not possible, but, of course, the normal safety precautions must be observed if such solvents are employed.

The technique which has just been described really serves to illustrate a principle, and it is worth experimenting with a number of contrasting substances in order to achieve a variety of effects of a similar nature. The success of any technique of this kind depends on the use of two essentially dissimilar substances; in other words, one which is soluble in water and one which is soluble in mineral spirit or alcohol, so that by using the appropriate solvent one of the substances can be removed without removing the other. There is, of course, a third consideration, namely the characteristics of the pigment to be used in the printing of the design. There would be little point in ending up with a stencil which was water-soluble if the ultimate intention was to print in water-based dye.

The reader may care to consult the list of substances and their characteristics contained on page 114 before proceeding to experiment along these lines.

Another technique for producing a positive stencil, which is in some ways similar to the one described above, makes use of the photo-sensitive properties of gelatine when mixed with potassium dichromate. Gelatine is the substance which has been used traditionally in the making of photographic stencils, although it has now been largely superseded by water-soluble PVAs (see page 48).

The first task is to coat a screen mesh with plain gelatine (mixed as suggested on page 116). To do this, the screen is tilted at an angle of about 45°, with its underside facing up. Using a large, soft brush or mop, warm gelatine is flooded over the mesh starting at the top and working systematically down the screen, never allowing the leading edge of gelatine to solidify. Readers with a knowledge of traditional water-colour painting technique will see the similarity to 'laying on a wash'. The aim is to fill the mesh completely with gelatine and to be certain that this has been accomplished, it may be necessary to repeat the procedure when the first coat is dry, preferably working from another edge.

Although the gelatine will solidify quite quickly as it cools, it takes a considerable time to dry and may need to be helped by a fan-heater. The design is then painted on to the gelatine in screen lacquer (ordinary Japanese lacquer purchased from a hardware store will suffice if it is not too thin). It must be remembered that one is working on the underside of the screen so that the design will need to be a mirror image of the intended final print.

Whilst the lacquer is drying, some potassium dichromate crystals should be dissolved in water (see recipe page 116). This solution should be brushed thinly over the lacquer and gelatine so that it is absorbed by the gelatine except where it is protected by the lacquer coating. There will be a slight tendency for the dichromate solution to creep under the lacquer unless it is brushed on very sparingly with a very soft brush.

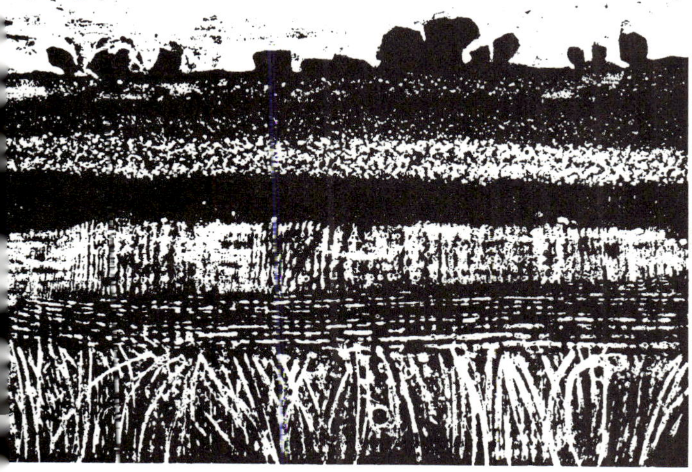

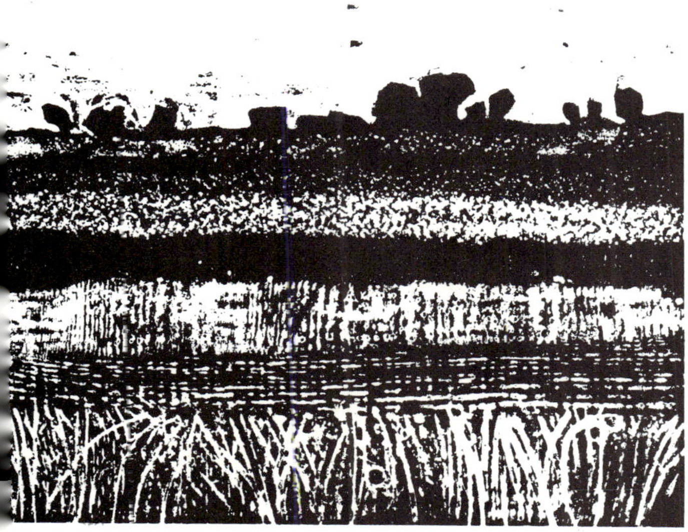

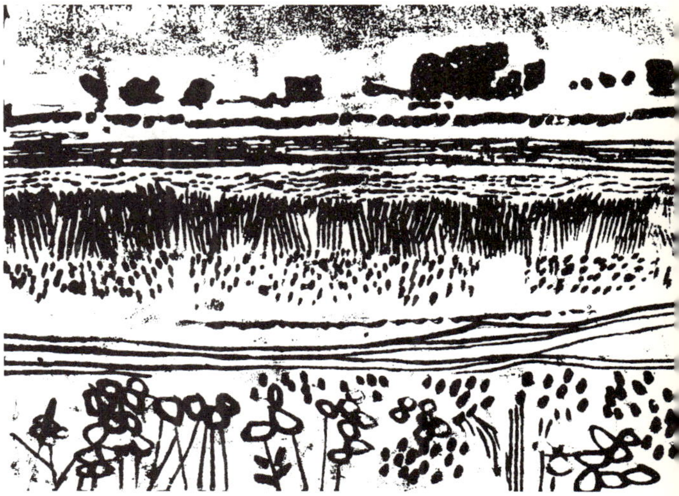

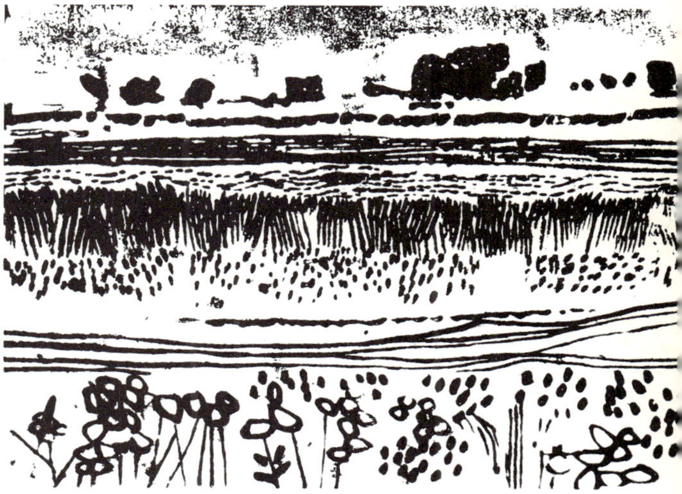

Three-screen print using wax rubbing (*top left*), wax rubbing and some wax painting (*centre and below left*) and wax painting made positive with a coating of gelatine and potassium dichromate (*right*)

The screen must then be left to stand in sunlight until the dichromate coating has turned from a bright yellow to a gingery brown. The combined effect of the dichromate and the light will by now have rendered the gelatine insoluble in water, except where it has been protected by the lacquer. When the screen is washed out in warm water the gelatine lying under the lacquer will dissolve away taking the lacquer with it and leaving a clear mesh in its place, representing the original design.

A screen prepared in this fashion will be very durable and can be printed in either water-based or spirit-based pigments. Before printing, however, it would be advisable to check the screen for 'pin-holing' which, if discovered, should be touched in with a suitable screen filler.

Proprietary stencil processes

The techniques described in the previous chapters have been of a somewhat improvisational character, designed to provide the beginner with a range of experiences employing, in the main, materials and substances which are available from non-specialist sources.

It has already been mentioned, however, that screen printing is an industry and as such, is catered for by active and specialised commercial suppliers offering extensive lists of chemicals, solvents and stencil products manufactured specifically for the craft.

Many of these products, particularly the stencils, are designed to satisfy very specific and demanding requirements and are consequently, fairly expensive.

One of the oldest and most commonly used of these stencil products, certainly in educational establishments, is the hand-cut stencil paper (*Profilm*) which consists of a laminate of shellac and paper. The stencil paper is laid over the design and fixed into place with adhesive tape, the design showing through the stencil as through a sheet of tracing paper. Using a very sharp knife, cuts are made in the lacquer film whilst ensuring that the backing layer remains intact. the parts of the stencil representing the open, or printing areas of the screen are peeled away from the backing sheet and the stencil is then transferred to the mesh by ironing with a cool iron. The original *Profilm* stencils are really only suitable for use with meshes made from natural fibres, but there are now many modern variations available which make use of synthetic materials and which will adhere to most types of mesh. The manufacturers of these stencil materials provide full instructions for their use (lists of manufacturers are included on page 119). From the point of view of the creative print-maker I feel, personally, that the use of hand-cut stencils is a rather laborious and mechanical process and that the kind of images reproduced by this method are often wooden and lacking in vitality. There is no doubt that in the hands of the experienced craftsman stencils of this type are capable of great accuracy and are very reliable for the production of posters and other graphic items where very exact registration is required. It can also be said that they do obviate the problem of 'saw-toothing' (see illustration page 56) which is a characteristic of liquid stencils.

One final word of warning about the use of all proprietary sheet stencils, including the photosensitive ones. They are all designed for very specific purposes and before investing in any sheet stencil material it is advisable to consult the supplier to make absolutely certain that the stencil one intends to purchase is the correct one for the particular job in hand, both in terms of suitability to the mesh and to the kind of pigment to be used.

General advice

It is generally understood that one learns from one's mistakes, but making mistakes can be expensive, both in terms of time wasted and in the cost of materials. The following are some 'do's and don'ts' which may prove helpful in the early stages.

1 Never print with a wet screen, ie a screen that has just been washed out with either water or cleaning spirit. If it is necessary to change the colour of the pigment during printing remove *all* unused pigment and wipe the inside of the screen clean with a barely damp sponge or cloth, depending whether it is a water- or spirit-based pigment.

2 Never leave a screen standing with pigment in it for more than a few minutes, particularly if the room is warm. Some modern inks are designed to be self-soluble so that the first pull with the squeegee after a period of inactivity should clear the screen but this is not always totally dependable.

3 Never stand a partially-cleaned screen at an angle against a wall. Streaks of pigment will run down over the face of the screen and these can be very difficult to remove. A screen which still has some pigment in it should always be stood nearly flat with just sufficient elevation at one end to hold it clear of the table surface.

4 Never try to make a print from a screen onto which some unwanted pigment has fallen. Always squeegee the unwanted pigment away onto a sheet of scrap paper before proceeding.

5 Do not be discouraged if the first print of a run proves to be unsatisfactory. A screen often requires to be 'run-in' on scrap paper before the printing proper begins. Remember that when printing with a screen in which the stencil is very open, one will use far more pigment than when using a screen in which most of the mesh is blocked out. Always make sure that there is sufficient pigment in the screen before making the print. This is particularly important in fabric printing where the dye being used is transparent.

6 Covered screens are fragile, store them carefully to prevent the mesh from dents or tears.

7 Be patient. Never try to print a screen until the stencil is thoroughly dry.

8 Avoid storing solvents in plastic pots which may themselves be soluble.

9 When experimenting, always take enough prints from each stage to ensure that one ends up with a reasonable number of completed examples. It is surprising how many prints get used up or spoiled in the course of a run.

10 Be aware of health and safety. Some substances used in screen printing give off fumes which may cause headaches or nausea and should only be used in well-ventilated rooms. Some of these substances are also very unkind to the skin and hands should be protected with heavy rubber gloves. Of course it goes without saying that inflammable pigments and solvents must be stored and used under strictly controlled conditions. Finally wax must never be melted without the use of a water-jacket and the level of water in the jacket must be constantly checked.

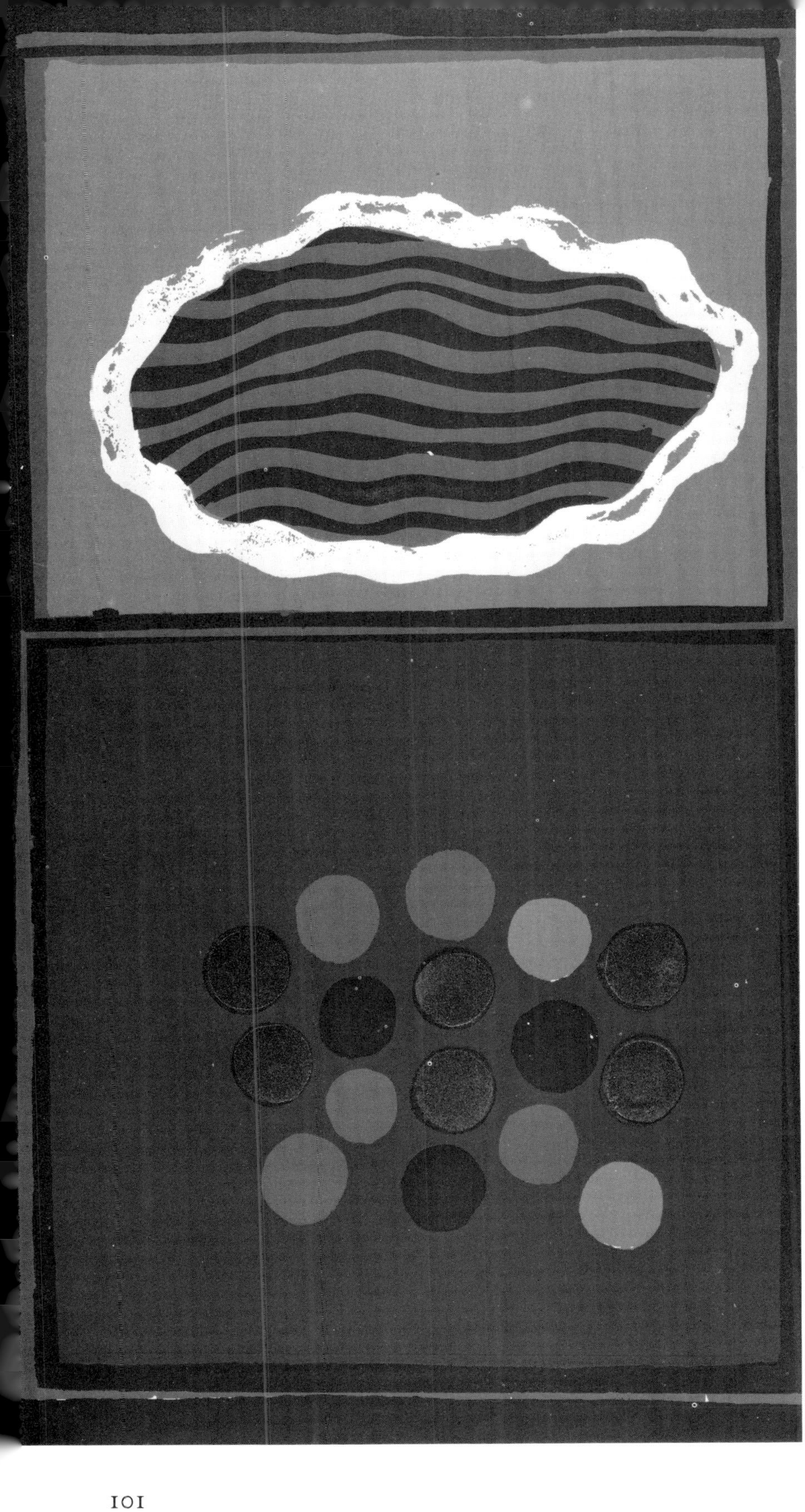

Left and overleaf Three variations on the same theme using the same and supplementary screens in different combinations

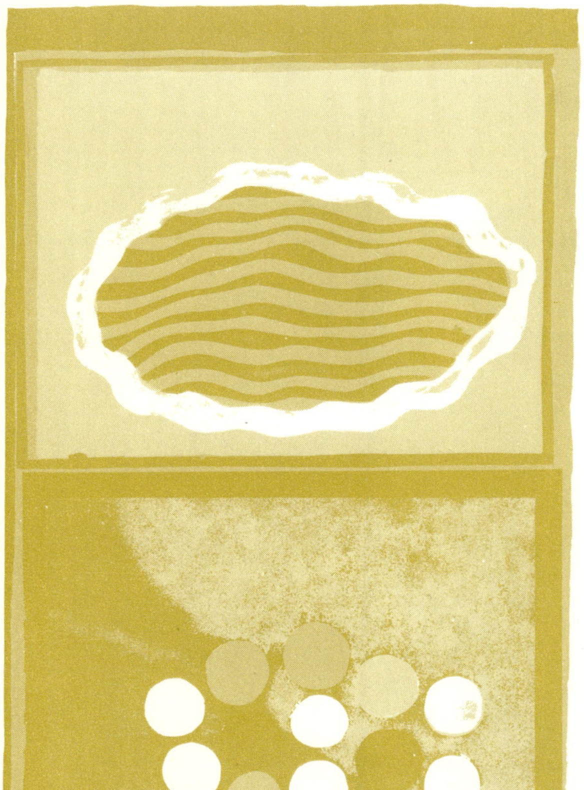

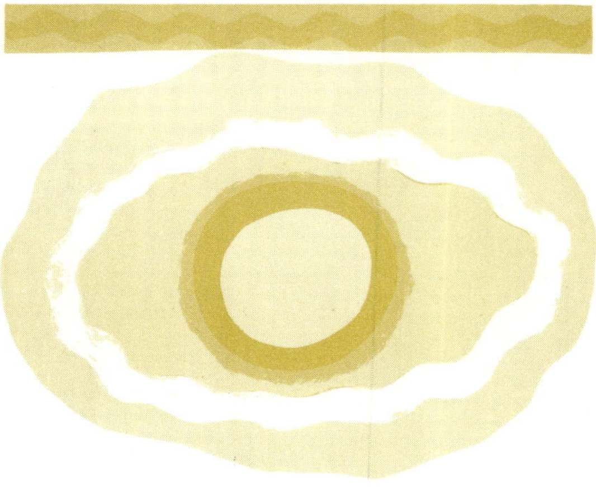

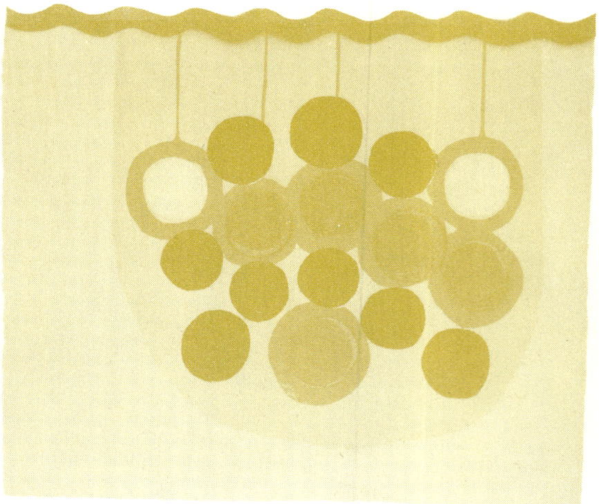

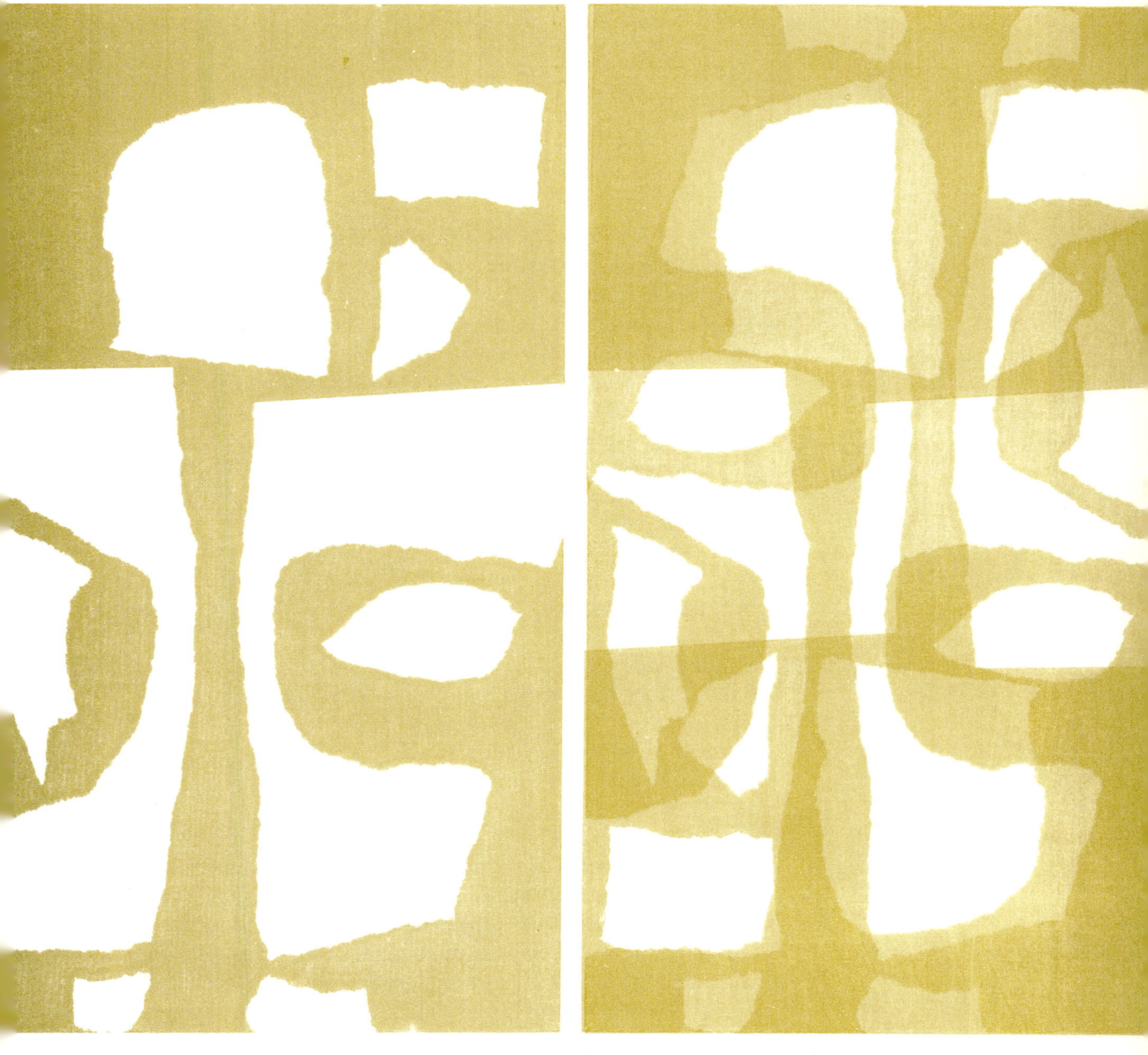

A print made by picking up newsprint shapes. The same screen has been turned round on itself and printed using the same dye

Summary of experiments

A work of art is much more than an exercise in techniques. A successful print is a form of artistic communication which exploits the characteristics of a particular process in the pursuit of an aesthetic goal. It must follow, therefore, that anything which is called an experiment in this book is concerned simply with developing the range and scope of technical possibilities at the disposal of the reader in his search for artistic expression. None of the experiments is in itself a formula for the production of a work of art. With this firmly in mind there follows a list which summarises the suggestions made earlier in the book and which can be used for easy reference.

Negative method

1 *Materials*
Brown paper gumstrip
Newsprint
Pigment in almost any form
Printing paper

Method
Mask the surround of the screen with gumstrip (unless otherwise stated this will apply in all the experiments). Arrange newsprint shapes on the printing paper, place the screen over the shapes and squeegee pigment across the screen picking up the shapes. The screen can be turned round on itself and an overprint made (see previous page). Shapes can be changed or rearranged at will, provided the pigment is not allowed to dry on the screen.

2 Materials

Brown paper gumstrip
Pigment (water-based for short runs, spirit-based for more lasting results)
Printing paper

Method

Cut gumstrip shapes and stick them to the underside of the mesh in the form of a design. Make several prints and wipe the screen clean. Add further gumstrip shapes to the design and overprint in a second colour. Repeat until a satisfactory result is obtained.

3 Materials

Water-based pigment (spirit-based can be used for short runs)
Paraffin wax melted in a water-jacket
Old hog hair brush
Printing paper

Method

Paint design in molten wax onto underside of screen mesh, making sure that the wax is always liquid by constantly recharging the brush. Print the screen, wipe clean and repeat until satisfactory result has been achieved. Wax can be removed completely or in part by ironing between sheets of newspaper.

4 Materials

Pigment (spirit-based)
Gum or water soluble PVA (or water-based screen stopper)
Printing paper
Strips of thick card (1 to 6 cm wide)

Method

Create design on the underside of the mesh, using the card to spread the gum. Lines can be produced by using the edge of the card. The card can also be bent to produce angled or curved marks. Make stage prints allowing fresh gum to dry thoroughly before each new set of prints.

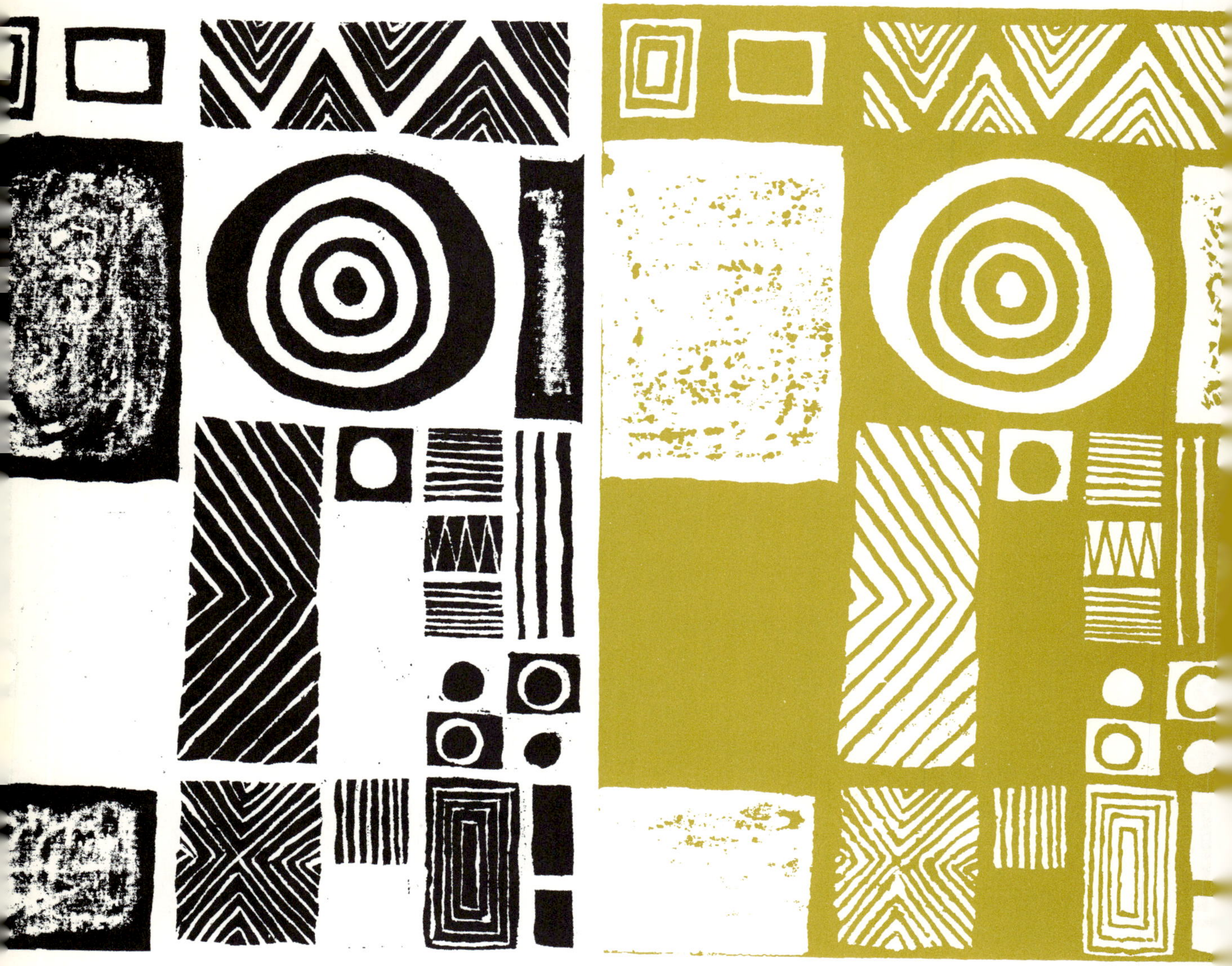

A 'negative' wax screen, mainly painted direct in molten wax but including some rubbing with solid wax (*left*). It was made 'positive' (*right*) by coating with gelatine and potassium dichromate and removing the wax

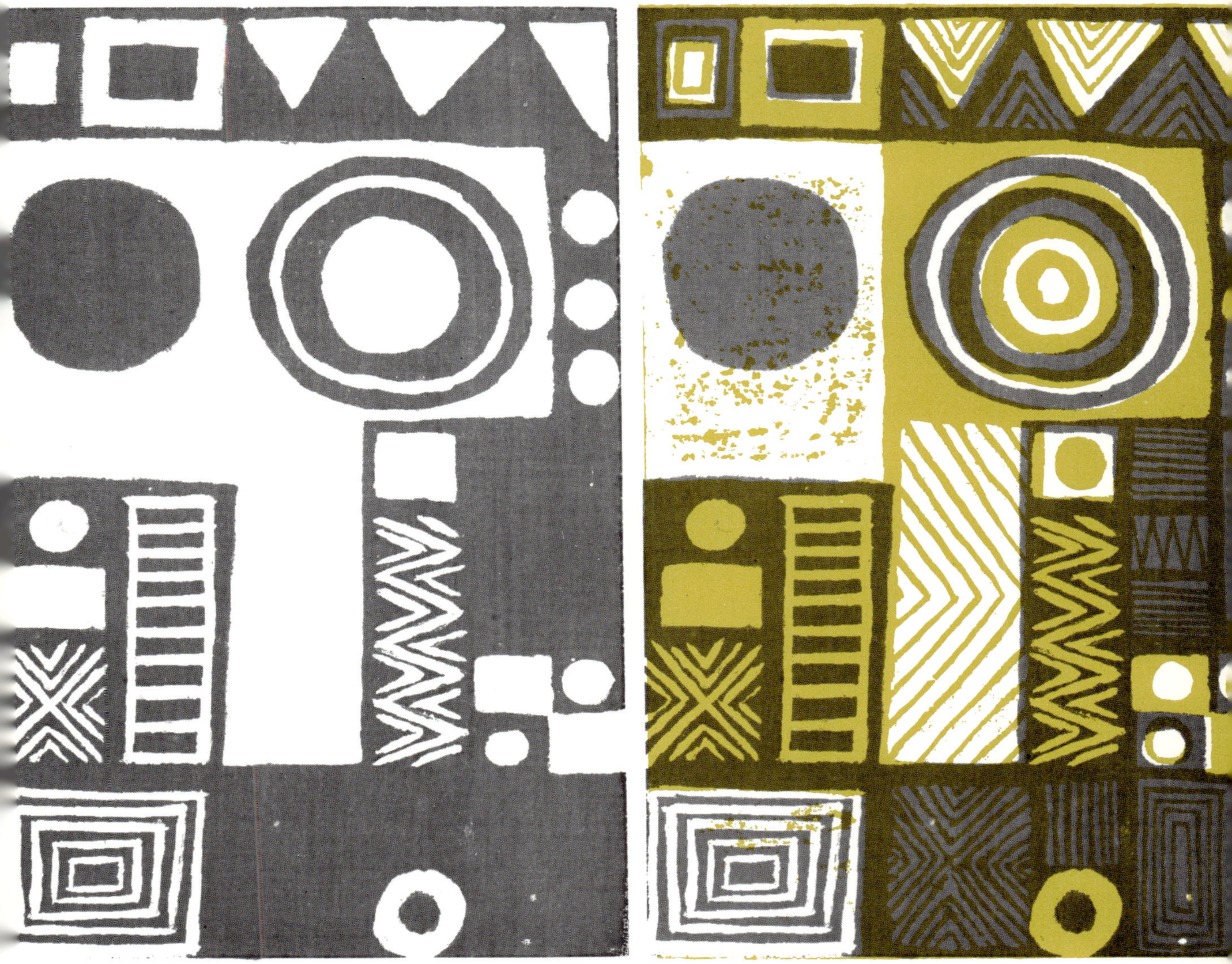

A supplementary screen was prepared in shellac (*left*) and superimposed in a second colour on the positive print (*right*)

5 *Materials*
Pigment (water- or spirit-based)
Lacquer
Printing paper
Sable or similar soft hair brushes

Method
This experiment demonstrates a method for producing a fine linear design and is, perhaps, the oldest and probably the most laborious way of transferring an existing design to a screen. The original design can be located under the mesh of the screen and traced directly in the lacquer, the mesh acting as a form of tracing paper. It is advisable to support the screen a few millimetres above the paper containing the design, to prevent the lacquer sticking the mesh to the design. A screen prepared in this fashion is long lasting and suitable for both water-based and spirit-based pigment since the lacquer is soluble in alcohol.

Positive methods

The following experiments demonstrate methods for producing a positive design on a screen, in other words the work done on the screen results in an open screen thus reproducing the original image.

6 *Materials*
Pigment (water- or spirit-based depending on the kind of final coating material to be used)
Paraffin wax
Hog hair or bristle brushes
Water-based coating material, eg PVA gelatine, gum, glue, etc. If the screen is to be printed in water-based pigment, standard PVA or PVA mixed according to the recipe for photographic processes on page 116 should be used.
Medium-sized paint or varnish brush.

Method
Prepare a design as in example 3, using molten wax. When the wax has set the screen can be coated with one of the glue substances mentioned above, using a paint or varnish brush. When the coating is thoroughly dry, the screen should be held up to the light to determine that no pin-holes of unfilled mesh

are present. Should there be any suggestion that the mesh has not been completely filled, another coating of glue is necessary. Finally the wax can be removed with a warm iron between sheets of newspaper or, when using non-water-soluble glue, the wax can be floated out in a bath of hot water. The screen will now be open where the wax had been and when printed will reproduce the original design. A similar procedure can be adopted using black waterproofing compound (asphaltum) instead of wax which is finally removed with mineral spirit, screen cleaner or possibly petroleum if safety conditions permit.

7 *Materials*

Pigment (water- or spirit-based)
Photographic gelatine
Potassium dichromate
Lacquer
Large soft brush for applying the gelatine
Fine sable or hair brush for the lacquer

Method

A screen is coated with gelatine ensuring that no pin-holes of unblocked mesh remain. When the gelatine is thoroughly dry, the design is painted on to the gelatine in lacquer. When the lacquer is in turn dry, a wash of potassium dichromate is applied over all. The lacquer will protect the gelatine from the dichromate so that when the screen is exposed to light the gelatine lying under the lacquer will not be hardened and can be washed out, taking the lacquer with it. The screen will now be open where the lacquer had been painted.

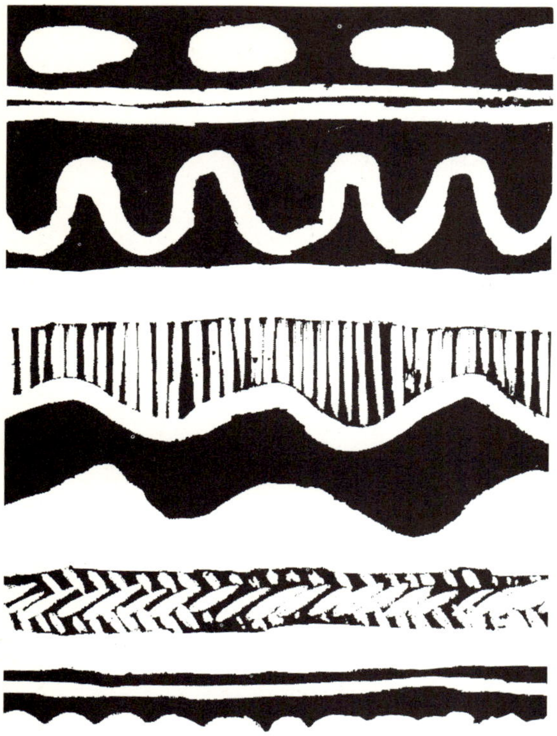

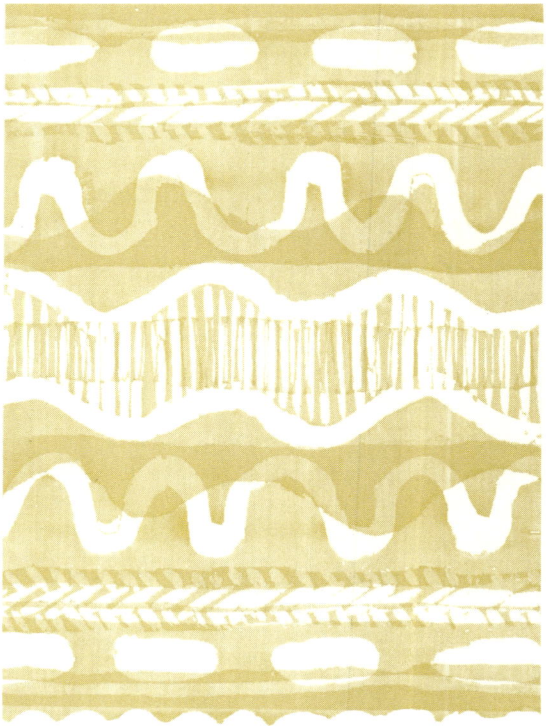

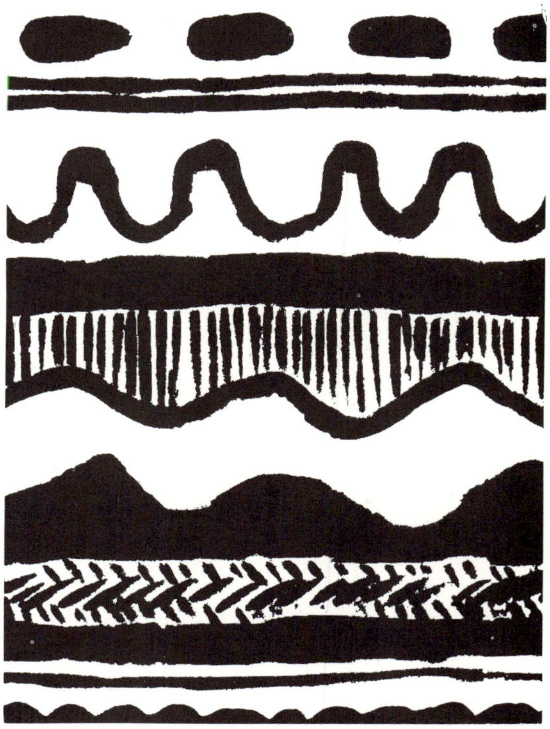

Design painted in melted paraffin wax directly onto mesh – in this case a course domestic terylene. Print in water-based dye (*top left*). Screen turned on itself and printed again in the same pigment (*top right*). Print from same screen after it had been coated in water-based gum and the wax removed (*below*)

Opposite A full colour diapositive (35 mm colour slide) was projected on to a screen coated with sensitised PVA (15 minute exposure) using a standard slide projector with a Q1 lamp. The resultant image was worked on in gum and painted over a second colour

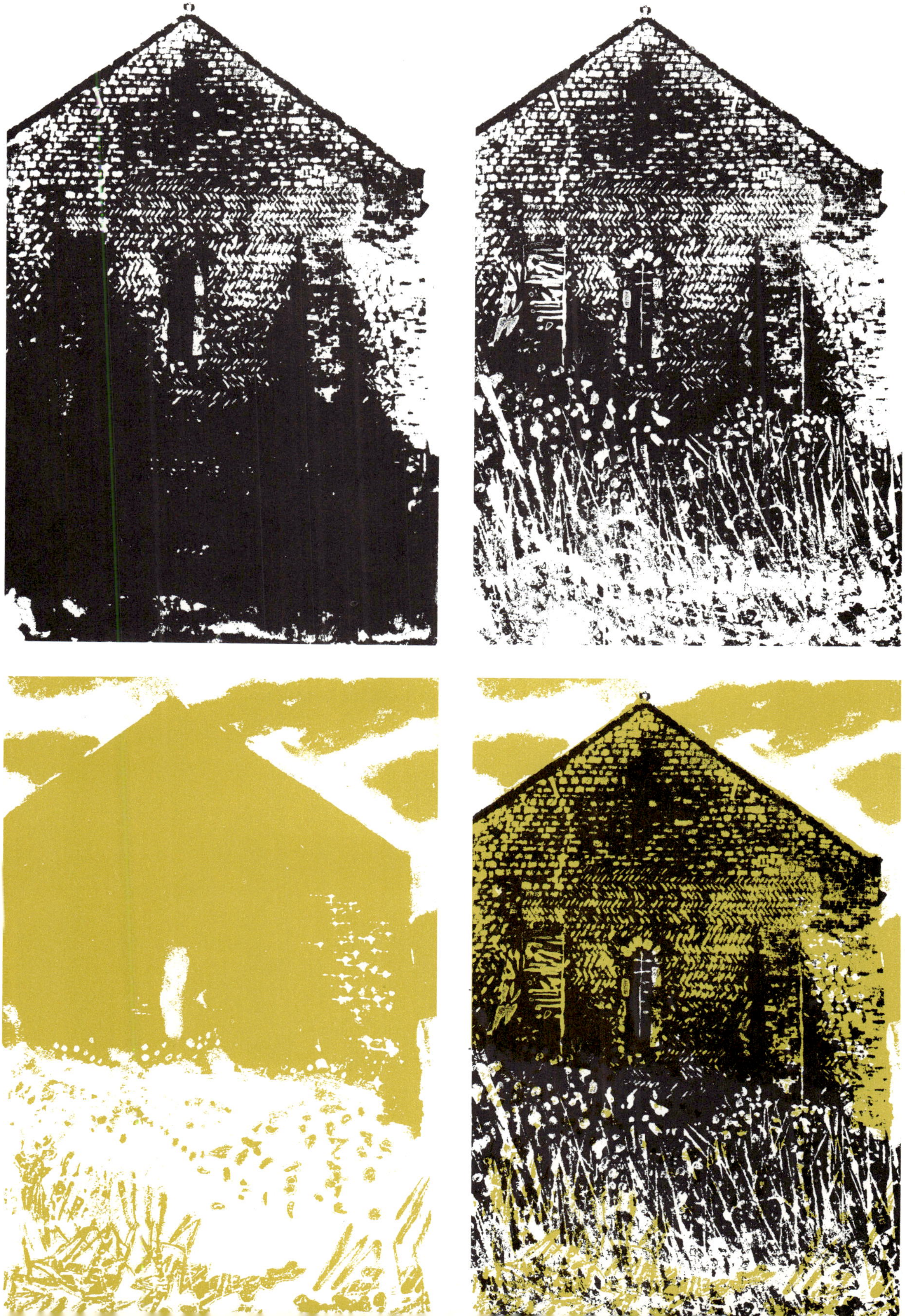

8 Materials
Pigment (water- or spirit-based)
Water-soluble PVA
(or proprietary direct photostencil emulsion)
Potassium or ammonium dichromate
Coating trough or squeegee
Light box or other exposure arrangements as described in the main text
Suitable transparent positive

Method
Sensitise the PVA as described in the recipe and coat the screen. Check for pin-holes and allow the screen to dry away from light Make up 'sandwich' and expose. Wash out un-hardened PVA, allow the mesh to dry and print.

These eight experiments do not summarise all the material included in the main text but should provide the reader with a range of experience which will provide a sound basis for further work. As with most crafts, experience develops confidence and it is advisable to carry out a number of trials and experiments before embarking on a major final project. Some things can only be learned by trial and error; the exact amount of PVA needed to coat a particular screen; the correct exposure time appropriate to a particular form of transparent positive, for example. It is a very good plan to keep a notebook in which is recorded information such as development times and ideas for different processes, etc.

Substances used in screen printing

Many readers will have had experience of the substances mentioned in this book in other contexts; but for quick reference I have drawn out the table of properties printed below. In very general, if rather unscientific terms, most of the substances used in screen printing can be classified under one of three headings according to the solvents employed in their preparation and use:

1 water based 2 spirit based 3 alcohol based

Some substances remain soluble in the original base liquid when dry, some require a different solvent at that stage and others can become virtually insoluble. It is therefore of the utmost importance to know the nature and characteristics of a particular substance. In this way disasters, such as removing a carefully prepared stencil with the first pull of the squeegee, can be avoided. The printmaker will also be in a much better position to exploit the properties of these substances to obtain useful visual effects.

In addition to the substances and materials which are more generally available, there are many proprietary products prepared specifically for screen printing which it would be impossible to include in the table below, not least because the list of such products is being added to constantly. Fortunately, many suppliers of screen printing materials provide very comprehensive information on their products and provided one is not intimidated by the rather technical character of these information sheets, they can be most useful.

Many other substances can be used to block out a screen if used as described above and can be experimented with provided that they satisfy the basic requirements; namely that the substance will dry in a reasonable length of time, that it is not dissolved by the particular pigment to be used in the printing, and that it can be removed from the screen at the end of the printing run.

SUBSTANCE	MIXED WITH/SOLUBLE IN	SOLUBLE WHEN DRY IN	EQUIPMENT CLEANED IN	POINTS TO NOTE
Gelatine	Warm (NOT boiling water)	Warm water	Warm water	Insoluble when mixed with potassium dichromate and exposed to light
Glue (animal)	Hot water	Hot water	Hot water	
Gum (arabic trag. British)	Warm water	Warm water	Warm water	
Polyvinyl acetate	Water	Alcohol (not easily)	Water, or when dry, bleach or paint stripper	Not too easily removed when dry. Liquid PVA can be washed out in water
Polyvinyl acetate (water soluble)	Water	Water	Water	
Shellac (white or button polish)	Alcohol	Alcohol	Alcohol	
Paraffin wax	Generally melted without solvent	White or mineral spirit, gasoline	White or mineral spirit	Care must be taken if using gasoline
Lacquer (oil)	White or mineral spirit	Not easily	White or mineral spirit	Paint stripper needed to remove dried lacquer
Lacquer (cellulose)	Special thinner	Not easily	Special thinner	Needs well-ventilated fire-proof conditions
Asphaltum	White or mineral spirit	White or mineral spirit, gasoline	White or mineral spirit	
Wax floor polish	Gasoline	Screen wash	White or mineral spirit	Useful as a more controllable alternative to molten paraffin wax when producing a positive screen
Screen filler (proprietary)	Mostly water based	Water	Water	Usually very quick drying, can only be applied with a spatula or strip of card

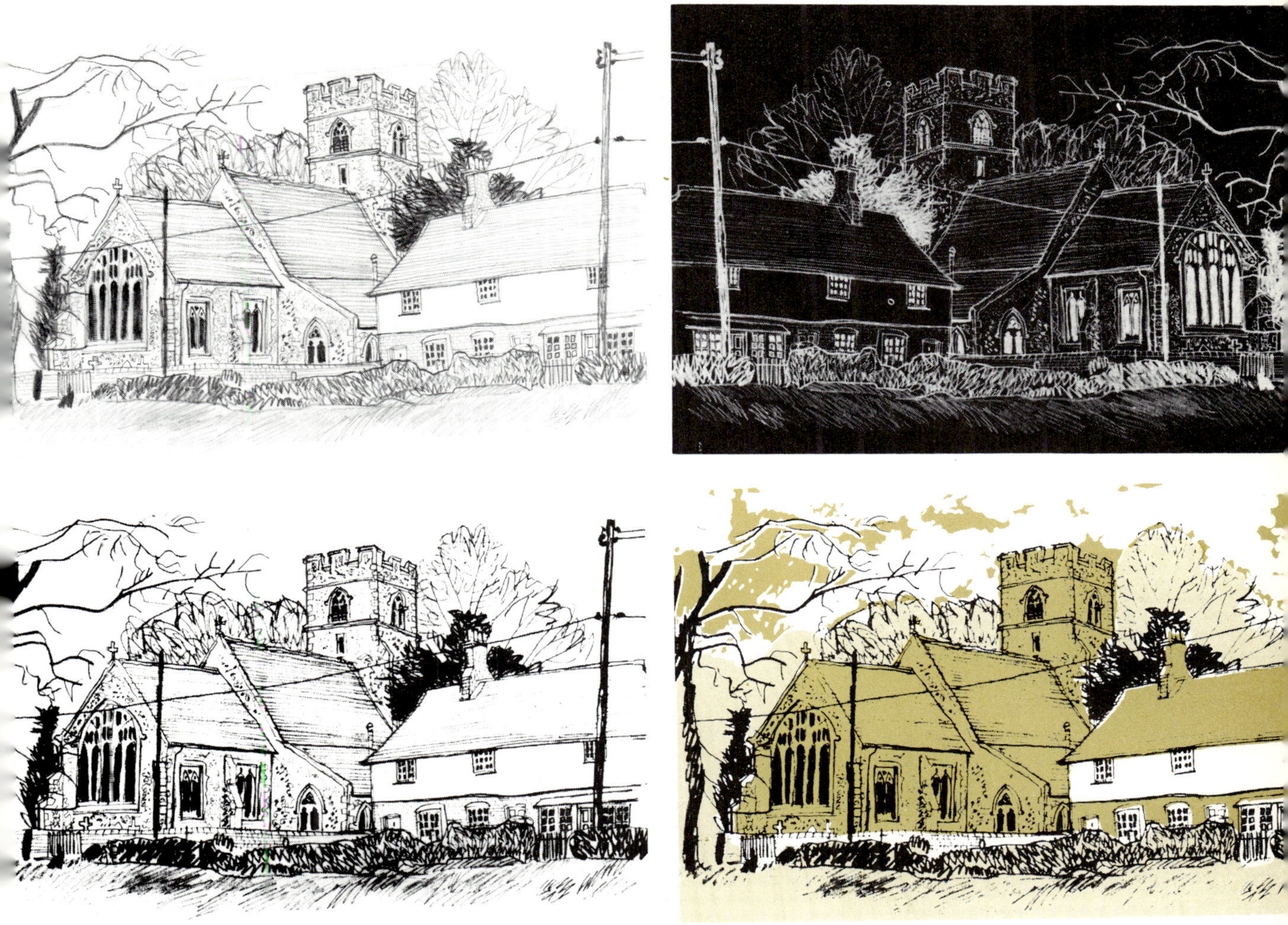

Sequence showing the development of a pencil drawing into a screen print by use of direct photo-stencil and addition of two hand stencilled screen for additional colours. Original pencil drawing (*top left*). 'Copycat' negative (copy made with office copier) (*top right*). 'Copycat' positive (*below left*). Finished screen print including second colour (*below right*)

Recipes

Recipes for most of the basic substances mentioned in the earlier text: it is assumed that most readers will prefer to work in everyday quantities and measures and these have been used throughout. The quantities given are approximate and can be varied to provide stronger or weaker solutions as experience dictates.

Glue, glue size (animal-based)

1–2 heaped tablespoons of granulated or powdered glue to 250 ml (½ pint) of water. Mix the glue into the water and heat in a water-jacket until completely dissolved. Do not boil or stir too briskly. Skim off any scum. Glue in sheet or cake form should first be broken up and stood in water overnight before heating. Glue should be used warm and if stored for any length of time, a little disinfectant added to inhibit fungus growth.

Gum (arabic, British, tragacanth, etc)

Prepare as above. Gum in lump form should be soaked before heating.

Proprietary gums

Tend to be a little thin for screen work and should be tested before extensive use.

Gelatine (photographic)

When mixed with potassium dichromate solution, photographic gelatine makes an excellent, fairly waterproof screen filler. As a material for photosensitive stencils, gelatine has been largely superseded by water soluble PVAs. Use 2 heaped tablespoons of gelatine powder to 250 ml (½ pint) of water, prepare as glue, *do not boil.* Can be reheated but do not store for more than a few days. A screen coated with gelatine and dichromate must be exposed to light before use with water-based pigments.

Potassium or ammonium dichromate/bichromate (stock solution)

Add one heaped tablespoon of crystals to 500 ml (one pint) of warm (not hot) water and dissolve thoroughly. Add to gelatine solution in proportion of 1:5 of gelatine. When using proprietary emulsions follow manufacturer's directions.

Polyvinyl acetate (PVA) white glue, water soluble

When using the water-soluble type of PVA as a photosensitive direct stencil, mix it with stock solution of potassium or ammonium dichromate in proportion of 5 of glue to 1 of stock solution. Experiment to determine whether the proportions should be adjusted one way or the other. Water-soluble PVA glues vary considerably in their composition and are in no way as reliable as direct stencil materials supplied by screen specialist suppliers. They are, however, very much less expensive and can also be used as a normal glue.

Cellulose wallpaper paste and dye powder

Mix paste to a thicker consistency than that recommended by the manufacturer. Dissolve the dye powder in a little warm water and stir into the paste mixture. Make sure all granules of dye have been thoroughly dissolved. Use as improvised pigment for printing.

Starch paste and dye powder

Can be prepared and used very much in the manner described above.

Shellac

Flake shellac should be just covered with methylated spirits (alcohol) in a sealed jar and allowed to stand for several hours until dissolved. This solution can be further thinned, as required, by the addition of more methylated spirit. Shellac can be purchased ready-prepared from hardware stores as: white shellac, french polish, button polish or patent knotting.

Lacquer

Should be used as supplied. Can be thinned with white spirit (mineral spirit) or recommended thinners but over-thinning will cause it to spread on the mesh.

Black waterproofing compound

Available as powder which should be mixed with white or mineral spirits, or in liquid form as one of the many compounds employed in the building trade.

Paraffin wax

Crumble solid wax into a container and heat in a water-jacket until liquid. Do not heat directly over a naked flame or even an electric boiling ring, as highly inflammable vapour will be given off. Paraffin oil can be added to prevent wax from setting too quickly but this will weaken the final film. It is preferable to use the wax very hot.

Health and safety

All human activities are attended by hazards of one kind or another and in the craft of screen printing, as in any other activity, the main rule must be to use one's common sense. However most local and national government authorities set out very strict rules for anyone engaged in commercial activities or responsible for an educational establishment.

It would be quite impossible to deal adequately with all the relevant rules and regulations in a book of this kind, but the following gives some indication of the problems that might be encountered and the precautions that could be taken to overcome them.

Toxicity

Many of the liquid substances used in screen printing are inherently poisonous and great care must be taken to label clearly all bottles and jars. This must be regarded as good studio practice, quite apart from any safety considerations. Most adults are unlikely to try to consume any of these substances and normal hygienic precautions should be sufficient to prevent food and drink from becoming contaminated. The fumes and vapours given off by many of the inks and solvents are another matter and great care must be taken to ventilate any spaces thoroughly where these materials are used.

It is also important to protect the skin and heavy protective gloves should be worn when handling the more powerful solvents. Screen wash is particularly hard, even on the toughest of skins, and should be treated with great caution.

Inflammability

Fire is always a danger with spirit-based inks and solvents, not only because the substances may catch fire whilst being used but also because any fire, whatever its origin, will be increased and made more difficult for the fire services to handle by large quantities of carelessly stored inks and solvents.

Rags which are used for cleaning should be disposed of at the end of each printing session or if stored for re-cycling, should be held in a fire-proof metal box. Smoking should not be permitted in the printing studio. Should it be necessary to use petroleum spirit (gasolene) as a solvent, this is best used out of doors.

It has already been mentioned that when melting paraffin wax, a water-jacket must be used to ensure that the wax never reaches a temperature at which inflammable vapour is given off.

The light from the UV lamp in the light box can be a source of danger, particularly to the eyes, and since it is not a good idea to be constantly switching the lamp on and off, commercially-produced light-boxes are fitted with a blind which can be drawn across the light in the box between individual exposures.

Bibliography

Biegeleisen, J.I., *Screen Printing*, Watson-Guptill, New York, 1971

Carr, F., *A Guide to Screen Process Printing*, Studio Vista, London, 1961

Chieffo, Clifford, *Silkscreen as a Fine Art*, Van Nostrand Reinhold, New York, 1967

Caza, Michael, *Silkscreen*, Van Nostrand Reinhold, London, 1974

Elliott, Brian, *Silkscreen Printing*, Oxford University Press, Oxford, 1971

Kinsey, Anthony, *Introducing Screen Printing*, Batsford, London, 1972

Kosloff, A., *Photographic Screen Process Printing*, Sign of the Times Publishing Company, Ohio, 1955

Kosloff, A., *Screen Process Printing*, Sign of the Times Publishing Company, Ohio, 1950
(both available from Sericol)

Middleton, H.K., *Silkscreen Process Production*, Blandford, London, 1967

Russ, Stephen, *Practical Screen printing*, Studio Vista, London, 1969

Russ, Stephen, *Setting Up In Screenprinting*, SEA, 1978

Schwalbach, M., *Screen Process Printing*, Van Nostrand Reinhold, 1971

Turner, Silvie, *Screen Printing Techniques*, Batsford, London, 1976: Watson-Guptill, New York, 1976

Turner, Silvie, *Handbook of Printmaking Supplies*, Printmakers' Council, 1977

Monoprinting

Marsh, R., *Monoprints for the Artist*, A Tivanti, London, 1968

Palmer, Frederick, *Monoprint Techniques*, Batsford, London, 1975

Graphic design

Chambers, E., *Camera and Process Work*, Ernest Benn, London

Cherry, David, *Artwork for Reproduction*, Batsford, London, 1976

Croy, Peter, *Graphic Design and Reproduction Techniques*, Focal Press, London, 1972

Green, Peter, *Design Education: Problem Solving and Visual Experience*, Batsford, London, 1974

Warford, H.S., *Design for Print Production*, Focal Press, London, 1972

Suppliers

Great Britain

Adelco Screen Process Ltd
Weydon Lane
Farnham, Surrey
Small hand-screenprinting tables

Alanden Printing Supplies
Clare Road
South Reddish
Stockport, Cheshire
Inks, squeegees, hand-printing units especially for schools

Argomatic Printing machinery Ltd
Hardman Street
Chestergate
Stockport, Cheshire
Large range of machinery from hand-printing frames to washing troughs

Autotype Co Ltd
Brownlow Road
London W13
Manufacturers of unsensitized films

Brico Chemicals Ltd
Bagnall House
55/57 Glengall Road
London SE15 6NQ
Water based Helizarin printing inks for fabrics

A G W Britton
27 Willow Way
London SE26
Printing inks

Candle Makers Supplies
4 Beaconsfield Terrace
London W14
Manutex, dye stuffs

Chaplin & Co Ltd
276 Camberwell Road
London SE5
Squeegee rubber

Cranco Engineering Ltd
Chapel Street
Long Eaton
Nottingham NG10 1EQ
Printing vacuum tables, printing-down frames, screen-washing units, metal screen frames, screen-stretching apparatus

Dane & Co Ltd
1–2 Sugar House Lane
London E15 2QN
Printing inks, squeegees, gauzes, films, printing tables, racks and miscellaneous supplies

Flock Coatings Ltd
Denham Way

Maple Cross
Rickmansworth
Herts
Flocking powders, flocking machines, flocking printing service

Fox and Offord Ltd
Alma Street
Birmingham B19 2RP
Compression moulding, transfer moulding and blow moulding machines

George Hall Sales Ltd
Hardman Street
Chestergate, Stockport
Cheshire SK3 0HA
Stencil products, photo emulsions and sundries

Graphic Display Products Ltd
Frogmore Road
Hemel Hempstead, Herts
Racks, vacuum beds, darkroom equipment and screen washers

Hall-Mark Machine Industries Ltd
Risley
Derby DE7 3SS
Small hand printing vacuum bed, squeegee cleaner

H G Kippax & Sons Ltd
Upper Bankfield Mills
Almondbury Bank
Huddersfield HD5 8HF
Semi automatic, hand-printing tables, screen washing equipment, printing down frames, pneumatic screen stretching equipment

John T Keep
15 Theobalds Road
London WC1X 8SN
Screen inks, pigments, varnishes and block-outs, extra strong retarder

E T Marler
Deer Park Road
London SW19 3UE
Inks, mesh, screens, stencils, equipment and machinery, vacuum printing tables, racks, squeegee dressers, stretching machines, screen cleaners

Peter Potter Products
Oliver Products Developments Ltd
Water Lane
Storrington, Sussex
Small hand vacuum tables, squeegee cleaners

A J Pollack
439–443 North Circular Road
London NW10
Complete range of screen printing supplies and stretching service

A J Purdy
248 Lea Bridge Road
London E10
Mesh, adhesives, chemicals

Pronk, Davies & Rusby (PDR)
90–96 Brewery Road
London N7 9PD
Complete range of screen printing supplies

Registerprint Machinery Ltd
360 Brighton Road
South Croydon, Surrey CR2 6AL
Svecia printing tables, squeegee dresser, fabric tensioner, small hand-printing tables

W J Reynolds (Equipment) Ltd
99–105 Leytonstone Road
London E15 1JA
Screen washers

Samco-Strong Ltd
PO Box 88
Clay Hill
Bristol BS99 7ER
Printing tables, semi automatic tables, exposure units

Selectasine Ltd
65 Chislehurst Road
Chislehurst, Kent
and
22 Bulstrode Street
London W1M 5FR
Stencils, squeegees, general supplies plus screen printing kits for schools

Sericol
24 Parsons Green Lane
London SW6
Complete range of screen printing supplies

Serigraphics
Fairfield Avenue
Maesteg, Glamorgan
Wales
Binders, solvents, screen fabrics, photo-stencils and equipment and kits for schools

Canada

Naz-Dar Canada Ltd
925 Roselawn Avenue
Toronto, Ontario
Canada M6B IB7
Complete range of screenprinting supplies

USA

Chicago Silkscreen Supply
882 North Milwaukee Avenue
Chicago, Illinois

Naz-Dar Co of New York
45-45-39th Street
Long Island City, NY 11104

Process Supply Co
986 Hanley Industrial Park
St Louis, Missouri

Screen Process Supply Manufacturing Co
1199 East 12 Street
Oakland, California

Silkscreen Supplies Inc
33 Lafayette Avenue
Brooklyn, New York
NY 11217

Index